The App... Organization

REVISED EDITION

By
Harlene Anderson
David Cooperrider
Kenneth J. Gergen
Mary Gergen
Sheila McNamee
Jane Magruder Watkins
Diana Whitney

Taos Institute Publications
Chagrin Falls, Ohio
USA

THE APPRECIATIVE ORGANIZATION

COVER ART: Photo by Kenneth J. Gergen of "The Gates," a Christo and Jean Claude exhibition, Central Park, New York City, February 2005.

REVISED EDITION
Copyright (c) 2008 by The Taos Institute

Library of Congress Catalog Card Number: 2007943488

Taos Institute Publications
A Division of the Taos Institute
Chagrin Falls, Ohio

ISBN-10: 0-9712312-7-3
ISBN-13: 978-0-9712312-7-6

PRINTED IN USA

Introduction to Taos Institute Publications

The Taos Institute is a nonprofit organization dedicated to the development of social constructionist theory and practices for purposes of world benefit. Constructionist theory and practice locates the source of meaning, value and action in communicative relations among people. Chief importance is placed on relational process and its outcomes for the welfare of all. Taos Institute Publications offers contributions to cutting-edge theory and practice in social construction. These books are designed for scholars, practitioners, students, and the openly curious. **The Focus Book Series** provides brief introductions and overviews that illuminate theories, concepts, and useful practices. The **Books for Professionals Series** provides in-depth works, focusing on recent developments in theory and practice. Books in both series are particularly relevant to social scientists and to practitioners concerned with individual, family, organizational, community, and societal change.

Kenneth J. Gergen
President, Board of Directors
The Taos Institute

For information about the Taos Institute and social constructionism visit: www.taosinstitute.net.

Taos Institute Publications

Focus Book Series

Appreciative Inquiry: A Positive Approach to Building Cooperative Capacity, (2005) by Frank Barrett and Ronald Fry

Dynamic Relationships: Unleashing the Power of Apprecitive Inquiry in Daily Living, (2005) by Jacqueline Stavros and Cheri B. Torres

Appreciative Sharing of Knowledge: Leveraging Knowledge Management for Strategic Change, (2004) by Tojo Thatchekery

Social Construction: Entering the Dialogue, (2004) by Kenneth J. Gergen and Mary Gergen

Appreciative Leaders: In the Eye of the Beholder, (2001) edited by Marge Schiller, Bea Mah Holland, and Deanna Riley

Experience AI: A Practitioner's Guide to Integrating Appreciative Inquiry and Experiential Learning, (2001) by Miriam Ricketts and Jim Willis

The Appreciative Organization, (2001, first edition) by Harlene Anderson, David Cooperrider, Ken Gergen, Mary Gergen, Sheila McNamee, and Diana Whitney

Books for Professionals Series

Horizons in Buddhist Psycholoigy: Practice, Research and Theory, (2006) edited by Maurits G. T. Kwee, Kenneth J. Gergen, and Fusako Koshikawa

Therapeutic Realities: Collaboration, Oppression, and Relational Flow, (2005) by Kenneth J. Gergen

SocioDynamic Counselling: A Practical Guide to Meaning Making, (2004) by R. Vance Peavy

Experiential Exercises in Social Construction — A Fieldbook for Creating Change, (2004) by Robert Cottor, Alan Asher, Judith Levin, & Cindy Weiser

Dialogues About a New Psychology, (2004) by Jan Smedslund

To order books online from Taos Institute Publications visit: www.taospub.net or www.taosinstitutepublications.net.

For further information on social construction theory, practice and ideas write or call: 1-888-999-TAOS, 1-440-338-6733, or email: books@taosinstitute.net, info@taosinstitute.net.

Table of Contents

Prologue

*The challenge for the authors of **The Appreciative Organization** was to draw from our collective experience in organizations, and then formalize an answer to this question: What are the central features of an organization if its practices are based on social constructionist ideas and Appreciative Inquiry? In effect, this book is born of two assumptions:*

From social constructionist perspective, we propose that what we take to be real, rational and valuable, are created through the people in relationship. The continuous creation and sharing of meaning is the most crucial ingredient in an organization's capacity to function in a rapidly changing environment. And, unlike command and control organizing, the process of appreciative organizing more fully engages and inspires the members of the organization and synchronizes the organization more precisely with its surrounding environment.

From the practice of Appreciative Inquiry, we propose that within acts of mutual appreciation, lay the seeds of relational vitality. Through affirmative interchange, dialogue is animated, value is generated, and life is injected into visions of the organization's future.

Appreciative Organization

In this book we focus on the challenges of contemporary life for organizations, the conditions favoring the creation of the appreciative organization, promising practices, and the fruits of organizing in this manner.

As founders and board members of the Taos Institute, we have worked collaboratively on this book. We are eager to share ideas central to the Taos Institute and to our colleagues who engage in various professional practices from Taos to Tibet. We hope that through your relationship with these ideas, you find your own creative impulses stimulated into action.

In closing, we wish to thank our Executive Director, Dawn Dole, for her constant encouragement and helpful commentary during the book's production. We also extend our appreciation to Sally St. George, Dan Wulff, and Robert Cottor, Taos Institute Board Members, and the Publication Committee, including Harlene Anderson, Jane Seiling and Jackie Stavros, for their reviews, comments and enthusiastic support of this project. Last, we wish to recognize the work of David Runk and his staff at Fairway Press for their courteous and efficient services as our printer.

Mary Gergen, Editor of the Second Edition

Chapter 1

Toward Appreciative Organizing

This book is designed to provide readers with the inspiration and resources for developing an Appreciative Organization, one that is maximally suited to the emerging conditions of the 21st Century. In this world of rapid and complex change, we believe the old hierarchically organized, command and control model of organizing has ceased to be effective. The process of appreciative organizing is optimally suited for the emerging conditions of organizations today. Needed is a new form of organization, more flexible, sensitive to change, and quick to utilize information. Such an organization is not only more effectively self-sustaining, but contributes to the personal lives of the participants and to the surrounding communities of concern. In this first chapter, we focus on conditions favoring a process of appreciative organizing. Simply put, appreciative organizing is based on the assumption that the continuous creation and sharing of meaning is crucial to the full engagement of individuals and to the capacities of the organization for fluid and effective transformation.

Organizations Under Stress

We are living in a period of enormous change. Whether we call it the "information age," the "Postmodern era," or "the context of chaos," there is broad agreement that times are rapidly changing. The force and implications of these changes can seem daunting, opening up possibilities of a self-fulfilling prophesy of helplessness and hopelessness that leaves us abandoned to a future of negative imagery. Consider some of the emerging challenges:

- Although often very large, organizations are increasingly fragmented — through geographic expansions, mergers, and the diversification of functions.
- In this age of technological innovations, information accumulates more rapidly, becomes increasingly complex, is less reliable, and is more rapidly outdated.
- The speed of change, in economic conditions, government policies, and public opinion, outpaces assimilation. Long term strategic planning becomes increasingly ineffectual.
- New organizations, new products, new laws, new systems of accountability, and new communication systems constantly shift the terrain of competition and cooperation.
- The diversity of differences — ethnic, cultural, ethical — involved in the creation of the organizational culture and its surrounds provides opportunities for growth and for conflict.
- Personal commitments to organizations diminish. Ties based on trust and long-term understandings are eroding. Company loyalty even seems "old-fashioned" to many young workers.
- The opinion climate can rapidly change, and the range of opinions to which the organization must be sensitive constantly expands.
- Demands for workplace democracy are everywhere increasing.
- The eco-geo-political climate, including global warming, ecological disasters, terrorist attacks, civil wars, govern-

mental shifts, and shifting political alliances all influence organizational activities in unpredictable ways.

These are major challenges to organizations today. How should an organization best respond to them? For many organizations the answer is one of life or death.

The Traditional Organization in Jeopardy

These dramatic changes in world context place the traditional organization under threat. Such organizations are established as solid structures, pyramidal in form. Orders move from top to bottom, information is passed in the opposite direction. Employees compete for upward mobility. Firm boundaries separate the organization from the world outside. Consider the challenges faced by such organizations:

- Those in command try to establish a singular and coherent view of *the* organization, its goals, and its practices. In the meantime, multiple views of the organization circulate both within and outside its walls.
- The CEO, executive director or president often is expected to provide the vision for the organization. Top down control undermines the initiative of those below to deliberate on the future of the organization. Their voices are lost, along with their desire to engage in renewing the organization's capabilities.
- Because the hierarchical structure heightens competition among members of the organization, they avoid cooperating with one another, unless it advances their own goals. Employees tend to pass on only that information which favors them.
- Diversification of functions generates ignorance of all that is not in one's assigned realm. Decisions within functional units are often self-serving, and are not coordinated with other groups in the organization.

- A stable organizational structure favors fixed flows of communication; differing perspectives may never confront each other.
- A strict boundary definition, distinguishing between what is inside vs. outside the organization, results in separating the meaning making process within the organization from the communities of meaning outside the walls. The organization runs the risk of blindness toward the cultures of meaning on which its future depends.

These are daunting challenges for the traditional organization. And, with the lack of alternative visions, the response to these conditions is too often a furtive clinging to the past. Steps are taken to strengthen the power of the few, clarify the policies and monitor compliance, sharpen evaluation of individual performers, and intensify the internal competition. It is precisely here that the potentials of the appreciative organization become relevant.

Enter the Appreciative Organization

The most common metaphor for describing the way a traditional organization functions is the human being. According to this view, the plans, goals, and decisions are made by the brain (at the top), and the actions are executed by the body (or the workers) below. There is much that is inadequate about this metaphor. Most importantly, it ignores the fact that all members of the organization have able brains as well as hands and feet. However, the way in which all of the brains in the organization function largely depends on relationships among the participants and others. These relationships can be stifling, or they can unleash enormous potential. If we understand the functioning of these relationship and set specific practices in motion, the organization can be transformed. The organization can charge ahead, ready to meet and master the challenging new world conditions. Four basic ideas provide the scaffolding for understanding the function of relationships in the appreciative organization.

#1 We live in worlds of meaning

Traditionally we think of organizations as functioning in the real world, made up of things like salaries, production lines, factories, and inventories. These are the realities of organizational life, and it is important to understand the way they function. Our perspective is quite different. In our view, organizations live or die not by virtue of these realities, but by the way in which realities are constructed. What some call "our leader," others may call "a tyrant": what some say is an "organizational ethic" others may say is "a ruse." The fact that objects are moved out of a factory does not in itself constitute "production." It all depends on what objects we are willing to count as a "product." The very same objects could be viewed as "marketable products" or as "waste products," depending on the meanings we assign. There are no "problems" in an organization except within a particular framework of meaning. One person's problem is another's opportunity. By taking this position, we replace the realist's view of "the world as it is" for the constructionist view of a "world that has meaning for us." It is through these constructions that the future of the organization depends.

****

Judy Wick, founder of the White Dog Café in Philadelphia, sets an example for other restaurateurs in her approach to ecological issues. Her menu specializes in ingredients from local farms, which she often subsidizes in order that they may operate according to high standards of production and animal care. The White Dog "garbage" is now recycled for fertilizer and the deep-fat frying oil is converted to diesel fuel. Garbage doesn't mean waste at the White Dog.

****

#2 Meanings are embedded in action

As the world has meaning for us, so do we act. To construct the organization as valuable, its goals as worthy, one's duties as reasonable, one's colleagues as esteemed, and one's identity as valued by others is to invite vigorous and productive engagement in organizational life. An example: if one's salary means that one is "underpaid" or "under-appreciated," it is more likely to invite lethargy or destructive acts than spirited dedication to the advancement of organizational goals. How one acts as a member of an organization is the outcome of meaning-making in the organization.

****

The chancellor of the college sends out a message following an honors convocation thanking members of the campus community for making it a success. Individuals and groups from the janitors to the food preparation people to the provost are included in her praise. Donors and students, as well as faculty members are lauded. The brilliant success of the event is attributed to them all. Each alone could have created nothing. This message plants fertile seeds for future undertakings as each member of the community feels appreciated and respected for their contributions.

****

#3 Meaning is constructed in relationships

The meanings we assign to the world are not our private inventions. They do not originate in minds cut away from others. They are created within our history of relationships — from our early childhoods to our most recent conversations. If there were not a world of conversation in which matters of "the economy," "fairness," "quality of life," and so on were focal, it is unlikely that one would ever use such terms. It is through our relationships — through talking, gesturing, and acting together — that we determine what is real and valuable for us. It is through relationships that rationality is created, goals become important, and one feels valued or not.

On Election Day, a father and his young daughter are shopping for groceries. The girl asks her dad to explain a poster she had seen in the parking lot advocating the election of a candidate. Her father says, "All you have to remember, honey, is to vote for the candidate with the shortest name."

****

#4 Shared meaning relies on appreciation

Meaning is born in the act of affirmation. If we speak to another, and there is no response we are left to wonder whether or not our words were heard. "Did he hear what I said? Has he misunderstood me? Is there something I don't understand?" Meaning comes to life when another affirms that our words make sense, when there is some form of "yes, I understand." Affirmation is a way of appreciating another as a meaningful agent. In addition, someone who gives affirmation is also invited into meaning-making. Failing to understand others leaves us with no means of participation. In effect, in affirming we also recognize our own entry into meaning. The process of co-creating meaning begins. Appreciation is the essential ingredient of coordination. Mutual appreciation ignites the growth and enrichment of meaning.

****

A multi-disciplinary committee was formed to help select a new head of a division on the basis of an external search. Included in the group were several mid to high level managers, and two administrative assistants, who would be working with the new hire. The meeting began by sharing a lunch together. During this time, at the oval table in the small conference room, a mix of light-hearted conversation and ideas for conducting the search process were discussed. There was informality, laughter, and a sense that people were "all in this together," despite the fact that it was beyond the call of everyday duty, and not normally a task for which anyone would volunteer.

Near the end of lunch, one of the more junior managers suggested that instead of going through the list one by one, in alphabetical order, people just said who their top picks were from the pile of 50 applications — just to see if there was any agreement. A consensus that this could be tried was informally achieved. The group around the table took turns naming their favorites, and someone volunteered to keep a tally on a white board. As it turned out, the level of agreement was very high. When there were differences people expressed their views as to why they liked one candidate or another. As the meeting progressed there was a growing sense of respect, appreciation, and rapport among the members of the committee. The chair participated primarily as a facilitator, who agreed to collect the names of the top five candidates and present them to the executive board for further deliberations. The meeting, which could have taken weeks, was concluded in two hours.

The appreciative atmosphere extended beyond the meeting and permeated the relationships of the committee members long after their assignment was finished. People who served on the committee developed a special kind of kinship, and they even suggested among themselves that they should become The Committee; whenever the organization needed to solve a sticky problem in short order, they could call on them. It was a shame, they thought, to lose the magic and the momentum they had created.

****

The Fruits of Appreciative Organizing

These four ideas provide direction for exciting transformations. We move away from a view of the organization as composed of a single head or leader, and a docile and passive body of supporters. Instead, we come to see organizations as enormous repositories of life-giving potential. Within every conversation, there is opportunity for generating mutual value, for incorporating new information and ideas, for creating harmony, and enriching the spectrum of possibilities for the organization.

Appreciative organizing brings benefits not often witnessed in the rigidly hierarchical organization. There is a continuous flow of meaning making throughout the institution. Relationships bring forth previously untapped resources for making sense with others. In particular, appreciative organizing bears the following fruits:

- *Innovation* — As views and values circulate more freely within the organization through all levels and functions, so are members exposed to many ways of understanding. As an attitude of appreciation is fostered, people listen to each other. And, as different ways of understanding are brought together, novel combinations are invited. Creativity doesn't spring from the head of the isolated individual; it is born in the intersection of different views.
- *Flexibility* — Through dialogue, new information is continuously being processed, and plans and practices are more sensitive to the changing situation. Because the concept of process replaces the traditional model of organizational structure, one is prepared for movement. Ersatz project groups can become powerful and sensitive centers of change within the organization. Movement, as opposed to "the single best structure," becomes a way of life.
- *Integration* — A successful organization is one that has integrated a diversity of viewpoints within its boundaries. Re-circulating identical opinions is equivalent to breathing stale air. If a diversity of ideas and information circulates

freely throughout the organization, parochial decision-making is reduced. Local decisions reflect ever-expanding domains of meaning. Depth of understanding is never sufficient for decision-making; breadth is also necessary.

- *Collaboration* — Because the growth of meaning always requires appreciative relationships, collaborative decision-making is favored. One understands the limitations of local realities and value commitments and the necessity of inter-dependence. To negate the other is to diminish one's own potentials.
- *Affiliation* — Because one works appreciatively with those in various levels and units of the organization, they become known as persons and their success becomes your success. They are not antagonists but protagonists in a story that you create together. Trust is pervasive.
- *Engagement* — Because each member of the organization recognizes one's interdependence with others, one becomes engaged in the trajectories of the organization. One doesn't sit and wait for orders, but proactively pursues organizational aims. As one helps to create the visions and their value, they become expressions of one's identity.
- *Coordination with the "Outside" World* — By increasing the range of dialogic participants and engaging with their diverse logics, the organization becomes more fully integrated with its surrounding culture. This allows for a greater affinity with the external community.

Building the Appreciative Organization

In the pages that follow, we will have much to say about the kinds of practice that foster appreciative relations. However, to prepare the way and to fill out the developing picture of appreciative organizing, the following invitations are especially important:

Foster Relational Interdependencies
Creating webs of interdependent relationship is a necessary

prelude to the development of a thriving organization. As webs of interdependency expand, so is the flow of meaning within the organization extended. This expanded flow not only helps to coordinate disparate groups around common goals, but as new views are shared the potential for greater creativity and flexibility is more easily realized. When any group becomes isolated — whether at the level of top management or in the mail room — there is danger of misunderstanding, a failure in coordination, and the generation of conflict.

****

A merger of a British and an American company was in process. It was clear to all concerned that the organizational cultures were very different. The Brits were more serious, refined, and polite, but distant toward strangers. The Americans were less sophisticated, but good at their crafts, and friendlier to outsiders. A consultant working with a merging engineering group decided to challenge them with the task of designing an apparatus that would be able to compete in a race. She created five mixed groups of US and British workers and set up the task. The firm provided supper, supplies, and space for the teams to work, which they did, late into the evening. The scene was helter-skelter, with engineers up on ladders, creating tracks across the ceilings, as well as crawling around on the floor putting together odd looking implements; there was much laughter mixed with intense brainy discussions, and collaborative creativity. At the end of the exercise there were winners and losers in the competition, but the new links forged across the "pond" were priceless.

****

Encourage Multiple Realities

In the Western world, we inherit a long-standing tradition of truth seeking. It is a tradition that strives to locate the most accurate and objective formulations possible, and to jettison the rest. Yet, from what we have said about meaning-making, there is no one truth about the world. If we approach decision-making in our organizations by seeking the one single inviolate truth, we are likely to eliminate many different perspectives. We settle on what seems for the moment to be "the real," and become blind to other perspectives, other traditions of meaning making, and the actions they invite. Through absorbing and reflecting upon alternative views, new syntheses are possible, and new realities entertained. There are multiple potentials to explore, but nothing is considered true beyond a doubt.

Promote Dialogue

We inherit a strong tradition of the heroic leader, one who thinks *for oneself*, and whose acts naturally inspire others to follow. However, our capacities to deliberate are also born in relationships. With multiple relationships, we acquire a greater range of concepts, rationalities, and images of the possible. Thus, as dialogue becomes a normal way of life in the organization, we grow sensitive to multiple realities and learn to negotiate across diverse relationships. Further, it is when ideas are shared, that they are generative. Replacing singular decision making with dialogue is essential to the operation of the appreciative organization. Further, when dialogue is appreciative it builds trust. The failure to engage in dialogue encourages alienation and suspicion; it is thus a counter-productive move.

****

A large pharmaceutical subsidiary is asked to operate more efficiently by its parent company. To facilitate this goal, the CEO engages with his team to create twelve groups of advisors, who are chosen from all parts of the company, and from all work groups, from managers to cleaning staff. Each group is charged with coming up with ideas to reach their goals. Because the groups are composed across disciplines and pay levels, relational interdependencies are created, intense and open dialogue is created, and a vision larger than the interests of any group is produced. Arbitrary downsizing was avoided through this process; instead new modes of productive activity were designed, which improved the bottom line of the company.

****

Encourage the Imaginary

Daily life in many organizations is concerned with putting out fires. The immediate challenges — how to meet this deadline, how to solve that problem, and how to avoid this disaster — are given top priority. Such issues can be all absorbing. When they fully consume our attention, the organization moves toward stasis. There is only a single reality before us. However, tapping into the imaginary allows organizational members to bring forth new ideals, desires, and visions for the future that inspires the growth of new meanings, new rationalities, and new actions. *It is within the dialogue of the imaginary that new worlds are brought forth.*

Act within the Moment

Change is inevitable. Holding too tightly to past constructions ("our established policy," "our five year plan,") fosters insensitivity to the complexities of the present. The traditional demand for consistency can be seen as an invitation to rigidity. Appreciative relations generate a condition of openness to new insights. Actors are able to move fluidly across the plane of possibility as the situation continues to change. This approach suggests that pre-planned responses to a crisis are only useful as one input into decision-making in a complex and chaotic situation. Planning is a useful exercise, but not the end-game.

Keep the Conversations Going

The firm, final, and fabulous conclusions of today often become tomorrow's delusions. To be sure, decisions must be reached daily in organizational life. People must act. However, these should be understood in terms of the specific conditions of the moment. Conditions never remain the same. Thus, it is important that actions remain continuously open for reconsideration. *Appreciative dialogue is never-ending.*

****

Bandits were marauding corporate offices in the semi-rural area outside a city in Latin America. The problem of dealing with this threat called on the innovative capacities of the employees, who needed to make preparations that would forestall the bandits emptying the vault, taking hostages or killing people. Discussions were held with all the departments so that everyone would be aware of the dangers and also of their potential responses if such an event were to take place. A "reasonable" amount of money was set aside for the robbery, the guards at the gate were advised not to engage in a shoot-out; the receptionist was to turn-over the money without protest. Thus, the organization had plans made in advance.

However, things did not quite go as planned and new initiatives had to be enacted. One night the bandits snuck into the building undetected; the next morning the receptionist was captured in the lady's room, and she became a hostage. Her colleagues stepped in to handle the negotiations, the robbery took place uneventfully, and the receptionist was later released unharmed at the gates. Tragedy was averted because the employees collaborated in a flexible manner in a dangerous and unique situation. Happily,

*through the coordination of the company with
external agencies, the bandits were later caught
by the police.*

****

What is Coming?

The remainder of this book outlines more fully how an appreciative perspective contributes to the strength and sustenance of
organizational life. In Chapter 2, we illuminate the process of
forming conversational partnerships, and its significance in the
life of the organization. In Chapter 3, we explore the concept of
leadership. An appreciative orientation places a strong emphasis
on collaborative leadership practices. Then in Chapter 4, we discuss in more detail the ways in which the entire organization may
be brought into the process of sharing and creating meaning
through Appreciative Inquiry practices. A new vision of evaluation in organizations is presented in Chapter 5, one that emphasizes appreciative relations as opposed to the critical judgment of
supervisors. Finally, in Chapter 6, we look at the relationship of
the organization to the world outside. Appreciative organizing
calls for an erasure of firm boundaries between what is inside and
outside the organization, and for a productive sharing of constructed worlds.

Focus Box

In this period of enormous change, traditional organizations are under duress; technological innovations create information glut; issues related to diversity grow with globalization; employee loyalty diminishes; and the eco-geo-political climate is unpredictable. Challenges to traditional organizations include the limitations of a pyramidal structure, with an invested hierarchy, firm boundaries between "us" and "them," and a communication pattern in which edicts flow downward and information rises. In order to meet these challenges, we envision a process of appreciative organizing.

The vision of appreciative organizing focuses on the collaborative process of constructing meaning. Meaning is born in acts of mutual affirmation. Such actions bring realities and values to life. Appreciative organizing favors the generation of interdependencies, openness to multiple realities; the promotion of dialogue among relevant partners; the development of novel and creative ideas; and conversations that are never complete. The benefits of appreciative organizing include innovation, flexibility, integration, collaboration, affiliation, engagement, and coordination with the "outside" world.

Chapter 2

Appreciation in the Meaning-Making Process

You receive a message from a senior official in your organization that says you must cut your expenditures by twenty percent. The message presents you with many options. For example, you can take immediate steps to cut your expenditures, you can delay action until you can "find out what this is truly all about," or you can interpret the message as "mere saber rattling." In effect, the order to cut expenditures isn't an order to cut expenditures until you grant it this meaning. It presents many options, and, as you make sense of the message and select an option, the message takes on one meaning as opposed to another. The senior official did not make meaning, nor did you; both the message and its interpretation were required. As mentioned in Chapter 1, the important point is *that making meaning is something we do with each other*. Meanings originate not within individual minds but within social processes. No single individual in an organization is in control of meaning; all participate — even in silence.

Not all meaning-making is nourishing. Bitter arguments and accusations contribute to meaning, although sometimes with disastrous consequences. Individuals and organizations live or die according to how the process unfolds. The major challenge, then, is to seek and cultivate those processes that contribute to effective meaning-making. Most particularly, what kinds of actions will lend themselves to appreciative organizing and vibrant organizational life? Let us consider these actions in terms of conversational partnership.

Toward Conversational Partnerships

Many relationships in organizations are primarily instrumental. People use each other to gain information, opinions, support, or to complete a job for which they will receive the credit. In contrast the appreciative process is non-instrumental, in that *conversational partners*, those who work together, engage *with* each other in pursuing mutual, not private, goals. Drawing from our collective experience, we see the following as pivotal to initiating, developing, and sustaining conversational partnerships.

Valuing the Other

Perhaps the key feature of conversational partnership is the capacity of individuals to value the other's participation in a conversation. When we think of meaning as originating in the minds of single individuals, we are often "fault finding." "What if their ideas trample on mine?" or "What if their plan is better than mine?" we might ask. When we realize that meaning is *co-constructed*, that it requires more than one to "make" an idea, then a premium is placed on mutual valuing as opposed to egocentric competition.

On a practical level, it is helpful here to cultivate a stance of *positive listening*. Positive listening refers to being attentive and respectful, conveying that you believe the other is a worthy participant in the conversation; allowing the other person(s) in the conversational space to fully express their views without premature interruption; offering curious rather than judging comments or questions; and attempting to hear and understand the other to the fullest. An excellent example of this is when Marty

Moss-Keohane, a talk show host, gently asks people to "Help me understand what you are saying" when she finds an opinion complex or disagreeable. Listening to the other from this stance grants positive meaning to the other and also suggests reciprocity; positive listening is encouraged in the other. The result is conversation through which areas of agreement may expand and areas of disagreement may "dissolve."

Cultivating "Not-knowing"

In the traditional organization, a premium is placed on individual expertise. The ideal manager should possess full knowledge, sound ideas, and clarity of expression. However, in a world of multiple opinions, reasons, and values, such singularity of expression is problematic. In contrast, conversational partnerships are encouraged by approaching relationships in a posture of "*not-knowing*." Not-knowing means employing a stance of genuine and intense curiosity and interest in the ideas of others. It also means being provisional, offering our knowledge or judgments not as final conclusions but as possibilities for consideration. Rather than entering conversations with preformed conclusions, it suggests giving others time and space for expression and the respect of being valued as someone who has something important to say.

Often when leaders enter conversations, they may have pre-established outcomes in mind. However, by cultivating a not-knowing orientation, they will typically find many other good ideas and insights in circulation. If the leader is open to new possibilities, the outcome will represent an informed fusion of meanings, and be an outgrowth of mutually valuing relationships.

Exploring Multiple Selves

Traditionally, we place a strong value on individual coherence. Good thinking is characterized by logical consistency and integration. However, when we realize that meaning grows from relationship, we also realize the shortcomings of this univocal tradition. In the contemporary world, we participate in an unprecedented array of relationships. As a result, we carry with us multiple and conflicting ideas, insights, and rationalities. We are both "liberal" and "conservative" depending on the situation. We prize honesty and yet we love tact. We sympathize with the plight of third-world workers, and continue to shop at the stores that sell their goods. These various viewpoints can be described metaphorically as multiple selves. A demand for coherence silences many of our inner voices, which are vital resources for our conversations. Conversational partnering is enriched by responding with and a sharing of these many selves.

In practice, this means one is capable of challenging any ideas, including one's own initiatives, in a conversation. "Here is one way of looking at the issue," we might say, "and there are other ways to understand this." It is often useful to treat offerings within a conversation not as "my property, which must be defended," but as "trial balloons" sent up to see if they will fly. If one does come into a conversation as a "strong promoter" of an idea, comments by someone else may help the conversation move to the point at which other options may also be considered. This can expand both parties' understandings and open room for "gray areas" to be considered.

Nurturing Narratives of "We"

When we recognize the co-constructed nature of the realities we create, our attention moves from the individual participants in a conversation to the coordination between them. Good decisions are mutual achievements. In later chapters, we shall have much to say about ways in which the unit of "we" can be brought to life. However, as an introduction, we wish to point out the importance in conversational partnering of narratives, most particularly sharing stories about "what we have accomplished," "how we faced a challenge," "how we managed through bad times," and "times when we worked and played well together." Such stories fortify ongoing relationships, lending them value or importance. When we draw from these narratives, we acknowledge the bond between us, which encourages trust and openness. Narratives also suggest means to ends and what the future may hold. They are the recipes for life in any culture.

****

Narratives of "we" are important, not only to small, face to-face relationships. They may be essential to the organization as a whole. For example, a warehouse of a large manufacturing company situated next to an important river caught fire. The chemicals in the warehouse were so volatile that the entire river was set ablaze. As a result, the river was contaminated; fish and other plant and aquatic life were destroyed. A great community outcry resulted. In response, the company not only cleaned up the local damage and restocked and restored the river where the fire occurred but revitalized the river upstream as well. The refreshed river became an asset for the entire region, and the company was lauded for its efforts. The corporation went on to publish the story as part of the permanent record of the organization. The original story, one of corporate shame, was transformed into one of pride and inspiration.

****

Much of the preceding discussion implicitly supports the value of *relational equality*, and in this sense favors current movements toward workplace democracy and organizational flattening. *Relational equality* is achieved when all people in the conversation have an equal right to contribute to the conversation. However, we also recognize the need in many organizations for hierarchical structures. All people cannot contribute to all decisions, and integrative or overview positions may often be essential. Yet, we need not equate hierarchy with the old-fashioned view of top down authority. Rather, managers may effectively shift from directing others' performances from above to performing with them, perhaps in the role of a facilitator, helping them to accomplish their goals. For instance, a division manager can cease being a boss who "gets others to do what I want them to do" to being a manager who invites them to engage together to produce coordinated achievements of the whole. This orientation encourages commitments to the group's activities that might not have otherwise existed.

Transformative Dialogue

In our view, good conversational partnering will result in *transformative dialogue*, a conversational process in which the actions of the participants combine *with* each other to create a new outcome — none of which could have been predicted at the start of the conversation. Through this process, meanings may be clarified, modified, expanded, contracted, confirmed, or disconfirmed. Innovative possibilities are produced. This form of dialogue is contrasted with the *monological conversation*, in which participation in meaning-making is lacking. Monological conversations are like skyscrapers standing side by side, without windows, doors, or connecting bridges. Nothing happens between them. In transformative dialogue, participants in a conversation are not the same at the conclusion of a conversation as they were when they began. In monological conversations, there may be moments of sound and fury, but nothing of consequence results.

****

"As a partner in a small hi-tech start-up, I often enter meetings with a pretty good idea of what I think is best. The future is clear for me, and I am also certain that my plan is best for everybody else. If I remain in this posture, it is also certain that the result will be disaster. Inevitably, it is my plan against the plans of my partners. Sometimes personal feelings get in the way. If someone else's idea wins out, I feel personally defeated, and I am secretly happy when their ideas turn out badly. On the other hand, if I enter a meeting with an open mind, eager to learn

> *what others think, and pleased by their inven-*
> *tiveness, the meeting sails along. Sure, I bring*
> *my pet idea with me, but I don't consider it my*
> *child. It's just an idea, and the important thing is*
> *that it gets added to the mix. It's the mix that*
> *means everything." (Personal communication)*

****

Transformative dialogue is enormously important to the via-
bility of the contemporary organization. Participants emerge
from conversations carrying not only what they brought, but also
aspects of their partners' views and values. They see the world
not only through their own eyes but also with the eyes of others.
Their understandings are enriched, and they become more flexible in their relationships. The point of transformative dialogue is
not to create an organization in which everyone agrees.
Differences need not be suppressed; within differences lie the
potentials for expanded sensitivities and new creations. Rather,
transformative dialogue enables participants to understand and
appreciate the differences and use the multiplicity of views as
resources to meet new challenges.

This conversational stance is especially vital in an organization's relationships with the "outside" world, as we will discuss
further in Chapter 6. Whether it is with customers, clients, or
competitors, this form of conversation facilitates increased
opportunities for cooperation, and lower needs for protecting
oneself from others. When conversational partnering is priori-
tized, its efficacy is maximized, and individuals are more likely
to flourish. A new sense of valuing the other, cultivating the "not-
knowing" position, exploring, and sharing our multiple voices,
and bringing to life new transformative narratives occur.

Focus Box

Meaning making is a joint endeavor. It is a social process. Engaging in an appreciative process of meaning-making requires conversational partners who work toward mutual goals. To develop a conversational partnership it is important to value the other's participation and to cultivate a "not-knowing" stance, which is one that combines a genuine and intense curiosity about the words of the other, with a willingness to resist final conclusions. Conversational partnering is enriched by responding with and sharing our many selves with another. Our many selves allow us to challenge our own presentations, as well as others. In conversational partnerships we value stories that emphasize our mutuality, our "we" stories of success and supportive relations.

Good conversational partnering results in transformative dialogue, a process in which new outcomes are created. In the appreciative organization, transformative dialogues allow members to accept differences and to consider diverse views as resources for meeting new challenges, especially those with the external world.

Chapter 3

Leadership as Collaborative Participation

Appreciative organizing favors a new paradigm of leadership. Replacing the traditional emphasis on individuals who command and control others, appreciative leadership is earmarked by forms of collaboration that expand participation in all aspects of organizing from hiring and scheduling to strategic planning and organization change. As a daily practice, and when focused on large scale strategic agendas, appreciative leadership makes use of people's capacities to create value filled visions of the future.

Collaborative participation invites specific practices of seeking to discover differences, highlighting unique strengths and abilities and bringing out the best of people in relation to each other. Collaborative participation is increasingly apparent today in the leadership literature and practice, with books on participatory leadership, participatory planning, and participatory decision-making increasingly visible. In our own work, we have observed a pervasive falling away from old paradigm leadership practices. We have watched as men and women alike invite their whole organization, as well as customers and vendors, into processes of inquiry and dialogue designed to foster collaborative planning and action. We have seen presidents, directors, and chief financial officers sit at tables along side front line employees and participate as equals in conversations leading to mutual learning and organizational innovation. We have witnessed women and men in positions of significant power saying, "I don't have all the answers and I trust we will figure it out together." We have seen people using their power, resources, and relationships to create opportunities for others to realize their dreams at work.

Collaborative participation is becoming more and more the norm in hospitals, schools, charitable organizations, and government agencies as well as businesses worldwide. For example, as a way of setting a direction for its next five years a private school brought together parents, faculty, administrators, board members, and students for two days of inquiry. Together the group of 200 engaged in rich discussion about strengths and possibilities alive within the educational community, and energized by the commitment that comes from participation, they created an innovative path forward.

We believe that collaborative participation is the key to leadership in the appreciative organization. How is this so and what are the chief characteristics of collaborative participation? This chapter opens the discussion.

The Relational Difference

Most theories of leadership, especially the "Great Man" theory, focus on the capacities of the individual — a set of traits or behaviors possessed by certain people more than others. Leadership continues to be described, taught, and practiced as a set of individual skills. Based upon a relational theory of organizing, collaborative participation offers an alternative way of making sense of leadership. Its defining element is that leadership is born through relationships. There are no leaders unless others are willing to work collaboratively with them, and there are no followers unless there are leaders who are willing to serve as the relational conduit for inquiry and action. Thus, apprecia-

tive leaders effectively invite others into relationships that oιჳ
ize energy, effort, and action toward mutually determined ends.
Thus, leadership, as an individual trait, is replaced by a concern
with patterns of relationship: inclusion, coordination, and co-construction. When these prevail, we move toward the appreciative
organization.

As collaborative participation, appreciative leadership can be
exercised at every level of an organization. Those occupying
senior positions have special opportunities to set the processes in
motion. However, any member of an organization can initiate and
support bringing collaborative participation into being in their
realm of existence.

Leading through Collaborative Participation

How is collaborative participation to be realized by organizational participants? In their book on appreciative leadership,
Diana Whitney and Jim Ludema present five appreciative leadership practices that represent the values and practices of appreciative leaders.

- **Being Relationally Resonant:** Those who aspire to lead
  should be sensitive to the "vibes" that others project. They
  should be attune to the relational assemblies that are coalescing and dissolving around them. Who is feeling included and who is feeling ignored? Are there groups coalescing
  against others? Are there apathetic feelings that require
  attention? Are there special affinities that might be produc-
  tively engaged? How do others regard my involvement in
  the group activities? What image am I projecting to others
  about who I am?

- **Engaging With Others in Co-Creation:** It is helpful to
  admit others into the inner-circle of your creative activity.
  The lone genius model is a myth; no one is truly alone at
  their creative best. Great achievements are the result of a
  confluence of factors, some of which are not even intend-
  ed. Credit for good ideas must be given and received by
  many.

- **Bringing out the Best:** Making others look good is a good way to look good yourself, and in addition brings much added value to the task as others attain peak performances. Publicly acknowledging the achievements of others enhances further successes.
- **Asking Generative Questions:** Questions control conversations. Good questions orient conversational partners in productive ways. Good questions produce the opportunity for a transformative dialogue to occur.
- **Building Hope:** The choice to create optimism over pessimism pays great dividends. Dwelling on the impossibilities of a situation and creating despair voids creative potential.

No one person can design an organization's future. Patterns of action are intertwined and created through modes of discourse. Action does not originate in one person, nor is peak performance possible on one's own. The values and practices of the leader influence the possibility of collaborative participation. In our experience, the following are among the most significant steps in developing appreciative leadership skills:

Seek out Stakeholders

Collaborative participation begins when people ask, "Who else should be included in a conversation, decision or initiative? Who are the relevant and affected parties? Who needs to be involved to create the most coordinated and mutually inspiring results?" It is also important to ask if anyone is likely to be startled or dismayed by the results of a decision, or likely to oppose a change of conditions; it is wise to include them in the dialogue and decision making process as well.

****

A small family medicine clinic was interested in improving the ways in which their new doctors became integrated into their clinic. In order to do this, they invited their patients to become

involved in redesigning this orientation. Patients
were able to bring their experiences and feelings
about being assigned a new physician into the
conversations. The resulting orientation was
much more patient-centered and even included a
small session where patients served as teachers
for the new physicians. When these stakeholders
were involved from the start of an initiative,
loyalty, engagement, and mutual respect are
enhanced.

****

While highly beneficial and recommended, it may not always
be possible to include all those who have a stake in the process to
the table. At these times, a collaborative orientation will invite
commentary from the point of view of those who are affected, but
absent. For example, in a project related to zoo management
sponsored by a nationwide animal care organization, the question
was raised, "Who will speak for the monkeys? How can we get
the voice of the animals in the room?" These questions led
animal specialists and animal caregivers to be invited to attend
the meeting and to join in dialogue with policy makers, journal-
ists, zookeepers, and animal rights leaders. Like the patients of
the family medicine clinic, those with direct personal investment
in the lives of these animals offered perspectives not otherwise
amplified. The mutually constructed strategy was much stronger
and more readily acceptable to a larger public as a result of the
inclusion of their voices.

Value Diversity and Difference

The *I Ching*, a well-known Chinese book of wisdom, defines
opposition as a necessary condition for union. In order for union
to come about there must be something to unite — an opposition
of forces. A similar principle applies to collaborative participation.

In order for collaboration to occur there must be a means of
bringing together, valuing and aligning the diversity of experiences, strengths and ideas that will inevitably exist among all the

relevant stakeholders. Valuing is an act of recognizing the worth, quality and importance of something or someone. It is to seek out the very best of a person, group or situation. Appreciative organizing thrives when diversity is valued, honored, and optimized for the benefit of the whole and when the process of valuing is amplified.

Collaborative participation invites specific practices of seeking to discover differences, highlighting unique strengths and abilities and bringing out the best of people in relation to each other. This requires a valuing stance toward inquiry and listening, described in Chapter 2 as the "not-knowing" position. Often we listen to others' ideas with a focus on the problems; what is it that we don't like? A valuing stance toward a speaker means searching for what is unique in what is said, and how it could make a contribution to the conversation. How might the offering, the experience, the strength, or the idea be helpful, creative, and significant? In this way, multiple positive contributions can be woven into final decisions, plans, and actions. Through this process of valuing, a rich potential that draws upon the best of many and renders that which is problematic irrelevant is collaboratively co-created. At the same time, participants will feel heard and represented within the organization's resulting policies and actions.

****

When leadership becomes a relational activity, organizations change. Employees in one company using these approaches were asked the question: "What's best in our current 'organization?' " Among the answers were comments about leadership: "The leadership is willing to open up 'big' decisions to the larger workforce, and to listen to people about what they need to do their jobs. They're not afraid of the answers they'll get. They're willing to take the risk that something new might come out!" As another put it, "Our organization encourages 'leadership' that

doesn't include titles. People with ideas are
encouraged to lead groups and to push their
ideas. There's support for self-organized com-
mittees and task teams, and for working together
as 'corporate citizens.'"

****

Align Strengths to Bolster the Organization

Collaborative participation flourishes when unique strengths, capacities, and interests are valued and when it is possible for people to experience and act upon both their uniqueness and their communal impulses. Drawing upon diverse strengths and interests is the lifeblood of collaboration. People become engaged and participate when they are able to talk about what matters to them, in ways that matter to them. And it is through inquiry and conversation about strengths and capacities that they are given full expression.

Leadership processes that recognize, apply, and align strengths characterize appreciative organizations. Conversations that acknowledge differences in skills, capacities, and interests are foundational to new ways of organizing. Job assignments based on strengths and interests leverage individual potential in the service of collective capacity. It is a win-win for members and their organization. Leaders that facilitate the creation of development plans aimed at enhancing capacity in areas identified as potential are well-rewarded with enthusiasm and innovation. As we will discover in Chapter 5, when performance evaluation becomes an appreciative process, people find renewed commitment for their work.

A paradox of appreciative organizing is: the more the focus is on the special nature of individuals in terms of their strengths, capabilities, and interests, the more they value the collective and are willing to strive for its well-being. The more people's strengths are enriched through being recognized by others, the more they realize they have resources to offer to the community, and they will do so.

Value Commonality and Community

While valuing differences, collaborative participation can also be advanced by seeking out commonalties among the differences. What are the common goals, aspirations, or values within a group? By focusing on commonalties, otherwise divided factions can come together in a positive way. Finding similarities among individuals increases their trust, shifts their focus from working antagonistically to joining in collaborative goal setting and activity. Leaders can be very instrumental in bringing forth the awareness of commonalities among disparate others. This approach is particularly valuable when the organization is challenged by external forces, especially by those regarded as antagonistic (see Chapter 6).

****

In facilitating a project called United Religions, the consultants decided that the emphasis on difference was already implicit in the joint meeting of over 400 religious leaders from the world. Their goal was to discover their commonalities while respecting their differences. An important event that helped achieve this goal was to invite each participant to bring something to the meeting that was a symbol of special significance to the person, and about which a story could be told. This exercise both allowed for differences, and at the same time suggested great overlaps in the symbols, stories, and the significance each item had for each person. Additionally, the effect of the activity was to assist the facilitators in discovering ways of aligning strengths among the participants.

****

Move Beyond Blame to Celebration

Leadership through collaborative participation means avoiding blame talk. Instead, valuing others means that when someone

makes a seemingly foolish or careless mistake, there are proba-
bly reasons regarded as good or justified that encouraged this act.
Rather than evaluating others as second-rate performers, it can be
more productive to explore the conditions out of which the
"second-rate" performance was generated. People generally do
what they feel is best from within the sense-making relationships
of which they are a part. For example, a new employee may make
poor choices from the vantage points of those in charge.
However, they are likely to be good choices from within the relational network of which the actor is a part. The employee may not
have been given the relational resources to respond appropriately,
from the perspective of the manager. When we blame others, we
risk alienating them from future engagement; our criticisms may
cause them to "shift blame" to others. Those who blame may
develop a misleading sense of superiority. When others seem to
act foolishly, it is also wise to consider how one's own actions
contributed to the debacle (also see Chapter 5).

Along with seeking to understand the relational context of
performance, we suggest a shift toward celebration. Encouraged
are rituals or special occasions for valuing the community of
participation. Small celebrations of the "we" should be frequent.
Group meetings can usefully be extended into social occasions,
enabling participants to explore their interests outside of the
workplace and to draw significant others into their relational
circles. Participants should also join in the process of planning
and initiating such valuing occasions.

****

*The Mardi Gras Parade in New Orleans and the
Mummers Parade in Philadelphia rely on clubs
whose members work the entire year to prepare
for their parade appearances. In New Orleans,
groups are called krewes. For one krewe, the
leadership form that has emerged reflects the
notion of collaborative participation. Meetings
are held at a local bar where ideas are generated and a consensus is formed concerning the*

year's theme. This theme is derived from a poll taken during the meeting (after considerable amounts of beer have been consumed). As is the custom in most krewes, the leader is considered the King, but in this krewe, he is elected, and his role is to serve as coordinator, not controller, of the activities.

The mission of this krewe is to criticize capitalism, and so they march not as part of the Mardi Gras parade, which they believe has become a commercial spectacle, but by interrupting the parade and joining it illegally, much to the delight of the crowd. Krewe members, wearing lewd costumes, carrying scurrilous signs and objects, and chanting provocative phrases, are thrown out of the parade by the police as soon as they are spotted. In this krewe, the members take on the distributed leadership mode used by street demonstrators and others who protest the hierarchical ordering of society with its traditional leadership forms.

****

This chapter suggests the emergence of a new form of leadership based on collaborative participation. It is a form of leadership that seeks first to include others, then to develop their strengths and capabilities, and then invites them to contribute to the common good. When people are affirmed in relation to one another, they speak up more easily, more creatively, and with a greater willingness to contribute what they can. Appreciative organizations emerge from the shadows of command and control hierarchical organizations through relational practices of inquiry, collaboration, and celebration.

Focus Box

Appreciative organizing favors new forms of leadership, which emphasizes cooperative participation in all organizational functions among members of an organization. Leadership is born in patterns of relationship; successful leadership thus requires inclusion, coordination, and positive co-construction.

Important leadership practices include: listening appreciatively to others, engaging with others in creative activities, asking generative or productive questions, emphasizing the possible over the problematic. In appreciative leading, it is important to seek out stakeholders who wish to participate in an activity; to value diversity and differences of opinion among stakeholders; to align diverse strengths of members of the organization; to value commonality and community by discovering similarities within diversity; and to move beyond blame to celebration.

Chapter 4

Appreciative Organizing in Action: Small Groups and the "AI" Summit

Most of us can remember a time in our lives when someone we admired — teacher, parent, friend, boss — recognized something exceptional about us. Perhaps someone appreciated capacities and possibilities in us that we were scarcely aware of ourselves. Such experiences can be life-changing. We suddenly see ourselves in a new and different light. For some, such a moment can cause us to rethink our own image of ourselves and our potentials or launch a lifelong career. Consider the possibilities of unleashing this kind of powerful force within the organization, not just at special times, but every day, through the relations that people in the organization have with each other. To inquire, every day, into those aspects of organizational life that bring out the very best in ourselves, our relationships, our organizational practices, and our futures — *This is appreciative organizing in action.*

The particular focus of this chapter is in how practices of Appreciative Inquiry (AI) are integrated into the ongoing life of an organization. Appreciative Inquiry is based on the belief that organizations grow, prosper, or perish based on the relationships of those who participate within them. Further, it is assumed that participants have deep-seated values regarding the kind of organization they would wish to create. The practice of Appreciative Inquiry is designed to help people discover and realize the potentials of this positive core. This view is in contrast to the more traditional conception of the organization as a machine, in which each individual is assigned a role, and is operated by those in charge. AI enables participants to build their future together in ways that bring them joy and a sense of commitment to the organizational goals.

AI should not be considered a special intervention created by consultants to change the future functioning of an organization, but a day-to-day process of participation from all parties — first, on the micro-level of daily group functioning, and, second, on the macro-level of whole-group organizing. In creating a "full voiced" organization, the attempt is to honor all the relations within it.

Appreciative Organizing in Small Groups

In thinking about small group functioning, much that we have said in preceding chapters becomes immediately relevant. To re-emphasize the major points, appreciative organizing keeps paramount these key ideas:

- valuing the communications of others,
- honoring diverse viewpoints,
- including all potential stakeholders in the dialogue,
- recognizing multiple selves,
- cultivating "not knowing,"
- nurturing narratives of "we," and
- moving beyond practices of blame.

Beyond recognizing these basics of appreciative organizing, we outline here practices of appreciative inquiring that are important within small groups, and then we will examine organizational transformation in the total system. This latter inquiry is called the "AI Summit," in recognition of the ultimately inclusive process that it is.

Creating Futures through Appreciative Inquiry

Appreciative Inquiry (AI) is often viewed as a specific practice of organizational intervention — a practice relevant to pivotal phases of organizational development such as a crisis point, a reorganization initiative, or the launching of a new plan. The spectacular results of Appreciative Inquiry used in this way, is well documented and evidenced in organizations large and small, profit making and voluntary, and around the globe.

Equally important, the principles of Appreciative Inquiry also provide a wide range of resources available for continuous use at all levels of human interaction — individuals, groups, and complex human systems. Appreciative Inquiry principles include:

- **Constructionist Principle:** An understanding and acceptance of the **social constructionist stance** toward reality and social knowledge; i.e., that what we believe to be real in the world is created through our relationships; through the conversations we have with each other, we develop agreements about how we will see the world, how we will behave, and what we will value.
- **Poetic Principle:** A valuing of **story telling** as a sensitive way of gathering knowledge about an organization, including the emotional experiences of its participants.
- **Principle of Simultaneity:** A realization that inquiry is change; the questions we ask are fateful in that an organization will turn its energy in the direction of a question, whether positive or negative; as a result, the seeds of change are embedded in the formulation of a question.
- **Anticipatory Principle:** Decisions and actions are based not only on past experiences, but also on what we

anticipate, what we think or imagine will happen in the future.

- **Positive Principle:** A belief that a positive approach to any issue is as valid and as fruitful as a basis for action as a negative approach; taking the positive stance is an antidote to cynicism and defeatism.

In the dichotomous language of the West, many groups define their mission as problem solving, as opposed to potential-seeking. Production is down, marketing is ineffective, the field staff is slow, the government is interfering, and so on. "Our job," the group believes, "is to solve the problem." In Chapter 1, we noted that when group members talk with each other, they begin to define what is real and important. Thus, if they focus on "the problem," the problem will continue to grow in magnitude and detail. Eventually, the problem can "fill up the room." As the problem gains in size and power, it can seem to become even more burdensome and intractable. Energies are drained, and the problem-solving groups become demoralized.

Appreciative Inquiry provides an alternative way to discuss those things that the group considers a "problem." AI suggests replacing "problem talk" with "possibility talk." Whatever happens in human systems is subject to being labeled according to the cultural norm of the group. If one group sees a situation as a "problem," another might describe it as a "possibility." If we notice that for each situation, there are multiple interpretations of how good or bad that situation is, then we can also notice that in every situation there are lessons to learn, knowledge to gather, and new experiments to try. "Problems" can be redefined and re-visioned.

A challenge to those who are used to regarding "problem solving" as essential to the improvement of an organization is this: "If all the problems in an organization were solved, would the organization be perfect?" Not likely, because it is not the *lack of problems* that creates powerful organizations. What energizes the participants in the organization are the visions of the possible and the opportunity of engaging in the pursuit of something valued or desired. AI places a strong emphasis on possibility talk as a way of moving beyond an undesired situation. In every kind of organization, such talk can become a key feature of group processes. As this mode of discussion becomes customary, attention is engaged, energies released, and morale is elevated; the group is able to move forward with enthusiasm.

****

Members of the faculty at the campus were complaining about the behavior of the students. They were late to class, were frequently absent, hadn't done their assignments, did poorly on exams, and seemed intellectually dead! The faculty leadership decided to hold a forum for the entire student body to outline these issues, and to warn the students to start behaving in a responsible manner. When the student government council discovered this plan, they requested a space on the program to voice their complaints about professors who were late in getting to class, who didn't return papers promptly, who weren't prepared for class, and who were basically boring.

For one professor, who was schooled in the ideas of Appreciative Inquiry, this entire project seemed headed for disaster. She went to the staff member planning the event and suggested that it might work better if the faculty oriented their presentations to describing their ideal students, and the students responded in turn with their favorite teachers' behaviors. The new organizational plan was accepted, and the meeting was held in an appreciative framework.

It was a smashing success. Stories of wonderful students and amazing faculty members filled the air; there was clapping and cheering from the assembly and each side was exposed to models of ideal decorum. Of course, the world did not change overnight but at least some progress was made and no bones were broken.

****

Integrating AI into Everyday Activity

Countless organizations have found they can change and grow through the use of AI during specially organized sessions. However, the principles behind AI can be applied every day within the organization. To facilitate this goal, the following features of AI are especially applicable.

Discovering Strengths

The traditional focus on problems often leaves a group blind to its strengths and potentials. The discovery phase in AI places a strong emphasis on exploring positive experiences, discovering in the past the roots of optimism, positive energy, and a sense of strength. The power of this exploration can easily be introduced into daily life in an organization. Time can be devoted to exploring past successes, resources that group members bring to the table, and/or times when the group has functioned effectively. In this way, the history of the group also serves as a model for what is now possible. For example, faced with the challenge of introducing a new product to the market, a group may revisit successful launches in the past and tell the stories of how good results were achieved. The significant elements of these stories will enter into the planning of the new launch, as well as increase the vision and energy of the participants.

Creating Visions

When we define the world in terms of "problems," we also narrow discussion to what can be considered "solutions." If "my problem" in a voluntary organization is "the irregularity of the volunteers' participation," my focus is narrowed to finding ways of increasing participation. In contrast, drawing from discussions of discovery, the group may be invited into expanding the vision of the desirable. Given the kinds of experiences that have brought life to previous relations, what kind of organization can be imagined at this point? What sorts of activities and challenges would now vitalize the participants? What would give them nourishment? Just possibly, such visions would also have a positive impact on volunteer participation in the future.

Designing Futures

Given a vision that brings the group to life, it is essential to pay attention to how it may be implemented. In this case, the kinds of group activities favored by appreciative organizing aren't fundamentally different from traditional planning. Perhaps the only significant difference derives from AI's emphasis on inclusion. Because group plans are likely to have an impact on many other people, it is useful at this juncture to broaden the range of participation. As preceding chapters have emphasized, can the vision be shared in such a way that there is broad "buy-in"? How can others add, expand, or sharpen the vision in such a way that it can yield success?

As an example, massive programs to halt the AIDs epidemic in Africa often have been unsuccessful, largely due to the failure to consult with the population under threat. Good ideas for Americans are not necessarily good ideas within the worldview of a local population in another country. The challenge is to include those who will be most effected by a decision into the decision-making process. For example, recently a project supported by former President Bill Clinton's Foundation, has been successful in distributing cheap and effective AIDs drugs to patients by working directly with privately owned local drugstores, an arrangement brokered by an African aid agency. In this way, the hoped-for future is one aligned with the needs and wants of the people with whom the future is being created.

Insuring Delivery

There is a strong tendency for groups to feel their task is complete once decisions have been made and responsibilities established. Yet, from the standpoint of appreciative organizing, we also recognize that every group member also participates in many other relationships, each demanding time and attention. Appreciative organizing calls our attention to the necessity of establishing future points of discussion, during which implementation and outcomes are considered. These discussions may be important as well in educating the group members about the way in which a given plan may be altered as it moves through various sectors of an organization. Their vision may be "morphed" in a variety of ways as other groups negotiate its potentials. Unless there is room for such "morphing," a plan can be based on information that may have seemed relevant at the beginning of the planning process, but is no longer appropriate to the situation.

Reflecting on Outcomes

While it is essential for a plan to insure delivery, the final activity invited by an appreciative stance is to reflect on the outcomes. In particular, we recommend that group participants come together after a plan is in effect to review its efficacy and impact. In part, this is a learning step; it is important to gauge the ways in which a shared vision has been fulfilled. However, it is also here that seeds are planted for the new stories or narratives that will give energy to future group discussions.

Appreciative Organizing: Challenges and Options

There are two key challenges to appreciative organizing. The *first* is nurturing the opportunity for groups of people to self-organize and the *second*, nullifying the danger of constricting solidarity, that is the tendency of self-organizing groups to become closed, autonomous, and dogmatic.

Toward Self-Organization

To the extent that appreciative processes are in motion, we can place strong reliance on self-organizing groups that is the capacity of groups to structure themselves in an effective, enthusiastic, and roughly democratic way. However, when directive leaders order what is to be done, there is a tendency to shut down self-organizing activities among the group members. Voices are lost, dialogic growth is curtailed, enthusiasm is reduced, and the participants carry little away with them to share with others. Sometimes they share resentment and resistance. In contrast, in many situations group members can create their own internal organization, draw from their own considerable resources, and generate excellent decisions to which they are committed. (Again, we emphasize the importance of appreciative processes to bring about these ends.) As we described in Chapter 3, the challenge for those in leadership positions is to be wise and agile enough to respond in an appreciative way. For tasks that require knowledge, support, and implementation by all the members of the organization, self-organizing is ideal.

The Dangers of Solidarity

There are potential pitfalls. Successful groups often come to see themselves as being all knowing and wise. There is danger when groups come to believe enthusiastically in the "rightness" of their decisions. Blinders are thus erected to other possibilities. The group can begin to function in the same closed-minded and non-collaborative manner often characterizing the leaders of old-style "top-down" organizations. In an environment of appreciative and relational dialogue, there are means of off-setting this tendency. Bringing in outside voices is one important step. In other chapters, we emphasize the need to encourage multiple and conflicting viewpoints, so that full stability is never achieved.

****

In one global organization in which we have consulted, senior executives were deeply concerned by the lack of coordination between the parent organization and their subsidiaries scattered across fifty countries. Many of the subsidiaries functioned in ways that pleased and fulfilled the goals of the local management without regard for the other groups. At times, the subsidiaries would even disregard directives sent to them by the parent organization because they felt the parent did not understand the local situation. Company executives, in turn, felt the subsidiaries were too parochial, and didn't understand the full business picture. Informed by appreciative thinking, the consultation focused

> *on a broad sharing of "best communication practices" between the headquarters organization and the subsidiaries. Plans were set in motion to create a method of operating based on these practices. The results of these appreciative interventions was to strengthen the trust and collaboration between the various entities of the organization.*

> **

Self-organizing seems to work best when people are guided by shared images of the future — i.e., vision, purpose, and goals. Once such shared images are in place, groups can work together in any manner, at any scale. Under these aligned conditions, there is reason to trust that the product of the groups' work will lead toward the fulfillment of the shared vision. Ways to development such shared visions in an organization are beyond the scope of this chapter. However, the discussion that follows describes one widely used approach.

Whole Group Organizing: The AI Summit

Imagine 2,500 people gathered at a strategic planning meeting, not there to rubber stamp decisions already created, but to co-construct new strategy, vision, and direction for organization's future — a pathway of generative and creative change.

This kind of large group would never be involved in such planning in traditional, top-down organizations. Conceived and planned at the highest levels, plans for change are initiated with a "communication roll-out" and are generally "pushed down" through the ranks. Traditional small group decision-making is based on the assumption that the most effective size for a planning group is six to eight people. Certainly small groups are more easily controlled, but the question today is, "Who should be present if we want to include all of the knowledge and innovative ideas within the organization?"

In the emerging organizations of the twenty-first century, it is imperative to break down the barriers across divisions, departments, and other organizational units in order to create a relational community capable of co-constructing multiple ways forward and to shift paths quickly in response to the barrage of information. In today's environment, and with proper planning, a group of 150 people can be more effective in strategic planning than a group of six to eight. If the purpose is to harness the collective group intelligence of an entire system, then a group of 500 people could be more effective than 150. These are some of the assumptions behind the large group method called the Appreciative Inquiry Summit, a planning method that often brings together the total membership of the organization — anywhere between 50 and 2,500 people — in a face-to-face session over a three to four day period of time.

Large group planning in the form of an AI Summit is one of the most exciting developments in the field of organization development today. The results can be dramatic. One key to a Summit's success lies in the integration of the organization — the crossing of boundaries, bringing together people from every level and function and from every stakeholder group. This may include customers who have a "stake," and external partner organizations. We have found that when people experience the wholeness and full voice of the system of which they are a part, they are motivated to contribute their best. Capacity for dialogue increases; creative visioning is heightened; enthusiasm ignited.

Appreciative Inquiry Summits have been conducted in factories, high-technology companies, consumer products organizations, medical centers, and universities worldwide. They have been used to craft breakthrough union-management partnerships, to facilitate mergers, to form strategic alliances between companies, to do annual strategic planning, and as an open forum for culture change.

****

At Nutrimental Foods in Brazil, the factory was closed for four days as they brought all 750

> *employees together, along with customers and suppliers, to create a new business vision using the AI Summit. A year later profits were up 200%; absenteeism was lowered by 300%; and the company now does this kind of summit every year.*
>
> *The same thing happened at Roadway Express, the second largest trucking company in the US. For two years, in their Chicago Heights terminal, Roadway brought over 200 people together for three days of strategic dialogue. Later, in their merger with the Yellow trucking company, they agreed that Appreciative Inquiry would be their way of conducting business and, as a result of that decision, regularly use AI Summits for business planning and implementation. Meetings included dockworkers, union leaders, and managers from every area, customers, truck drivers, and people from other benchmark companies. In this case, the breakthrough work had to do with letting go of fifty years of adversarial relationships. Everyone was invited into the top level financial analysis of the company's books; into creating changes in dock layout and customer products; into forging a new labor-management partnership; and into the re-design of the company's stock plans and decision-making forums. Innovation and increased profit is the continuing result of their collaborative practices.*

****

The AI Summit brings into sharp focus the relational basis of organizational life. Organizations are, first and foremost, centers of human relatedness. Relationships come alive where there is an appreciative eye, when people see the best in one another and the whole, when they share their dreams and ultimate concerns in affirming ways, and when they are connected in full voice to create not just new worlds, but better worlds.

Focus Box

In the appreciative organization, Appreciative Inquiry (AI) is integrated into the ongoing life of an organization. In small groups, appreciative organizing depends upon valuing communication, encouraging diversity of viewpoints, including all potential stakeholders in dialogues, recognizing multiple selves in people, cultivating "not knowing," nurturing narratives of the "we," and moving beyond practices of blame. Specific AI principles include:

1. The Constructionist Principle: that reality is created through conversations,
2. The Poetic Principle: that places a value on story telling,
3. The Principle of Simultaneity: that views asking questions as fateful in creating the direction of change,
4. The Anticipatory Principle: that sees visions of the future influencing decisions and actions, and
5. The Positive Principle: that views an optimistic stance as a fruitful alternative to cynicism and defeatism.

Practices that are encouraged by AI include fostering modes of discovery, creating visions of the future, designing new futures, insuring delivery, and reflecting on the outcomes.

Two important functions that must be met in an organization to fully function appreciatively are to nurture opportunities for people to self-organize, while nullifying dangers of closure in the self-organizing groups.

In the AI Summit, an entire organization can be brought together to create new futures. The success of a Summit depends upon crossing organizational boundaries, including all levels of stakeholder groups, and encouraging all participants to give voice to their views. AI Summits realize the relational basis of organizational life.

Chapter 5

From Evaluation to Valuation

The evaluation of individual performance is an unquestioned part of organizational life. Rituals of evaluation are not only regular and expected; they are typically required. How else, we ask, can we know if individuals are contributing to the organization's mission? Indeed, we believe that if we were to abandon evaluation, many individuals would cease to be motivated and their work quality would deteriorate. But, how accurate is this assumption? Is it true that performance would really suffer without individual assessment? Or, is the reverse possible? Might assessment even be injurious to effective performance? Perhaps both sides contain a grain of truth. Within this chapter, we are going to propose a shift from practices of evaluation to what we call valuation. In the appreciative organization, such valuing should play a central role.

First, let us consider the possible negative effects of individual performance evaluation on organizational life:

- **Fear of Evaluation:** If we are worried about others' evaluations, we may behave in ways that are likely to gain approval, and especially the approval of those who evaluate us.

- **Looking out for #1:** When we are evaluated, our personal welfare is placed in jeopardy. In this way, evaluations encourage us to look out for ourselves first. What is good for relationships or the organization as a whole becomes a secondary concern.
- **Others are a threat:** Individual evaluation stimulates the sense of competition. In this way, others' good performances can be seen as threatening. What if others are rated higher than oneself? When threatened by others, one may even try to undermine them.
- **I am autonomous:** Individual evaluation emphasizes individual autonomy. "It is I," we come to believe, "who must ultimately make decisions and act upon them." To accept others' opinions suggests that one is too weak to think for oneself.

It is difficult to imagine a world where evaluation is dismissed. Our need to know who and what is pushing our organization ahead seems vital. Yet, evaluation processes are typically focused on the competencies or incompetencies of individuals. Even an organization's attempt to consider working groups in the evaluation process (i.e., working teams, departments, levels of management, and so forth) generates an aggregate of the individual members of the particular relational unit being reviewed. The challenge we confront is how to move the review and evaluation processes away from an individual focus on achievements and toward an appreciation of the relational processes that are meaningful and useful in the organization. Ultimately the well-being of both the organization and its participants will depend on processes of coordination as opposed to the autonomous actions of individuals.

****

An example of the "survival of the fittest" mentality regarding evaluation is a method advocated by Jack Welsh, former CEO of General Electric. As he proposed, in every department, evaluators

> *must rate a certain percentage, e.g. 10%, of the employees as superior and give them large incentives to remain in the corporation, through raises, promotions, and other perks. They should fire the bottom 10%, and give average grades to the remainder. The organization should continue this policy every year until the under-performers have been eliminated. This mode of evaluation keeps everyone on their toes, according to Jack.*

****

As we see it, creating an appreciative organization requires a major shift in organizational posture: from evaluation to valuation. The term "evaluation" means "to determine or fix the value; to determine the significance, worth, or condition of something," often in comparison to a fixed standard or to other people. It means that one may always be found wanting, short of perfection. In valuing, however, the emphasis is on that which is esteemed. It is an inquiry into the positive contributions of the person to the relationships making up the organization. When this valuing orientation is dominant, the following tends to occur:

- We recognize that we are valued by others.
- We communicate openly and enthusiastically.
- We go "the extra mile."
- We are willingly accountable with others.
- We become more trusting and valuing of others.
- We are more willing to take risks.

These are all contributions to the individual's functioning within relationships. However, these contributions can also be recognized in outcomes at the level of the group.

- **Flexibility of Action:** Traditional evaluation attempts to apply a given standard across all circumstances of action. Yet, as many groups realize, the common standard does not always apply. In fact, not only may its application be dysfunctional, there is no incentive for "thinking outside the box." In the appreciative organization, different segments are liberated to translate the aims of the organization into different forms of practice. If carefree innovation is valued in one segment, smooth-running teamwork might well be valued in another. These differences are not treated as competing but rather as contributing to the efficacy of the whole. In place of the stability and uniformity of the traditional organization, the appreciative organization finds ways of integrating ingenuity.

- **Engagement in the Organization's Future:** Traditional evaluation brings one into consciousness of self: how am I progressing, what is my future? When a process of valuing is set in motion, there is a shift from concern with the self to the relationships of which one is a part. It is not so much "my welfare" that is central, as "ours." With the significance of good relations foremost, the way is prepared for significant investment in the organization's future. The shared visions of the future also ignite creativity in constructing action plans.

- **Flow of Information:** When one feels in competition and under potential with colleagues, there is a reluctance to speak out, to share ideas and information with others. The appreciative organization engages in valuing processes where members are continuously inviting each other into productive and engaging performances. In the appreciative organization, one member's success is every member's success, and information is more likely to flow easily from one sector to another.

- **More Sophisticated Decision-making:** As proposed in preceding chapters, the greater the participation in decision-making, and the more willing participants are to be open, the more informed the organizational decision. When participants feel that their opinion is valued, even if it does not conform to the common view, more active and informative discussion is likely to occur. Decisions may not be clear-cut, but they will be more sophisticated and subject to continuing scrutiny.

Now we turn to the question: What would the shift from evaluation to valuation mean in terms of practice? Innovative initiatives are invited in two major arenas: valuing persons and valuing relationships.

Valuing Persons

In our experience, the following are some of the practices that can usefully move an organization from an evaluative to a valuing posture:

- *Invite organizational members to share what it is about their job they do well and enjoy doing.* Periodic questions of this sort will keep in the forefront the wellsprings of value for the individual, as well as their contributions to the organization.
- *Ask peers and supervisors to share what the individual does best and what he or she contributes to the organization.* Communicate these opinions to the individual. Learning how your colleagues value your presence can be enormously powerful.

****

Diana Whitney and Amanda Trosten-Bloom have described their work with a company merger. The new CEO was a man with enormous energy and drive, inspiring, but also threatening. Inter-group relations were also unsteady. He asked the consultants to facilitate a retreat that would foster new conversations about the company's future. The session began with the request that participants share a story of professional success. The success could be large or small, significant or insignificant, as long as it was a moment in their professional life when they felt good about their work. After telling stories in small groups,

> *the team gathered to discuss them. As they lis-*
> *tened to one another, they began to recognize*
> *how much they appreciated each others' skills,*
> *resourcefulness, and enthusiasm. They also sug-*
> *gested that future celebrations of their joint*
> *achievements would be valuable to the organiza-*
> *tion's productive capacities. As a result of this*
> *mutual valuing, they were able to generate a*
> *platform of trust from which new possibilities*
> *could spring.*
>
> ***

- *Ask individuals to describe those talents and strengths they bring to the organization, and how they may best make use of these in their work.* In this way, members communicate to others what it is that can be appreciated in their work.
- *Work in groups to discuss how best to support each other in reaching performance goals and objectives.* Here individuals become sensitized to specific ways they may work together more effectively.
- *Ask individuals to discuss the help or support they receive from those with whom they closely work.* When these statements are shared with others, they contribute to productive bonding.
- *Acknowledge the time spent building positive relationships across levels, divisions, and locations.* This is valuable to the organization as a whole.

Do we dare to replace evaluation rituals with those of valuing? Here the skeptic begins to ask, "With all the emphasis on valuing, how will people learn about their shortcomings, those aspects of performance that must be improved? Don't people need critical feedback to improve?" These are good questions, and there is no reason we should abandon critical feedback altogether. However, we must again recognize that rituals of evaluation are born of distance and distrust. They inform a person that he or she may not be acceptable, and that continued scrutiny is necessary. In contrast, the valuing process invites the individual into a relationship of trust and security. In our experience, relations of this sort bring out the best in people. When individuals are valued, they will become more sensitive to those ways in which their work falls short in the eyes of others. Rather than being resistant or resentful, they will endeavor to correct their deficiencies. In other terms, rewards almost always bring forth better performance than punishments. Is it not worth taking the risk and moving toward a valuing posture in organizational relations?

Because errors and mistakes in judgment are human, they will not be eliminated through valuing practices — or any other. However, even mistakes may be valued as opportunities for improving performances.

****

Athletic coaching at the professional level often takes the form of severe and negative evaluations. Coaches are famous for being cruelly evaluative, especially after a loss. Reporters and commentators love to add their criticisms as well. Not enough is known about how valuing might induce better performances in players. Yet, as Brian Dawkins, Philadelphia Eagles defensive player said after a squeak-by win, 21-19, over the Washington Red Skins, "We have things we need to work on. I'm always willing to work on things after a victory. After a loss, we still have to work on things, but you'd much rather be working on those things after you win." Valuing is about winning; evaluation is a losing proposition.

****

Valuing Relationships

Traditional evaluation focuses on the competencies of individuals. As we propose, organizational realities, rationalities, and motivation grow out of relationships. Indeed, relationships are the font of all that is meaningful and valuable to the individual. It is important, then, that the valuing process also centers on relationships within the organization. Drawing on our own experience, here are a number of practices that may contribute to the valuing of relationships:

- *Invite individuals who work together to share stories about successful experiences in groups in which they have worked and how the groups succeeded.* Invite discussion on how the present group might realize some of the ideals embedded in these stories.
- *Invite colleagues to share their visions for ideal relationships within the group and ways of being together they would find optimal.* Invite the group to explore how they might realize these ideals in action.

****

A consultant working with the faculty of a large department at a private high school designed an appreciative process for evaluating the departmental curriculum and the faculty's delivery of that curriculum. The faculty, however, was entrenched in long-term conflict and factions and had no agreement about assessing themselves or their curriculum. Their earlier attempts to evaluate and re-design their course offerings and their mode of implementation had only created more animosity among the various factions within the department. Recognizing the potentially volatile nature of employing a standard evaluation process, the consultant met individually with each faculty member to learn about

*his or her high points as a teacher, as a member
of their particular department, and of the particular
school. Each faculty member was asked to think
about what might help the program evaluation
be as successful as possible. The consultant took
their suggestions and developed a retreat agen-
da that everyone agreed was generative in moving them toward evaluating and re-designing
who they were as a group.*

****

- *Invite pairs of individuals who work together to evaluate
  how their relationship functions best.* When is their relationship most productive? How might they find ways of
  bringing about these times on a more consistent basis?
- *Invite people to describe what it is they prize about being
  a member of a given work group.* Have them share these
  valuings with other members of the group.
- *Invite people to consider how they function as a group.*
  Under what conditions does the group thrive? Under what
  conditions is it threatened?
- *Invite groups to collectively acknowledge exceptional
  group functioning.* For example, supplement announce-
  ments of "the employee of the month" with "the group of
  the month."

The appreciative organization thus shifts attention from the
individual to the forms of relationship out of which zest, creativity, sophisticated thinking and planning emerge. Each of these
practices can contribute to just such goals.

360 Degree Valuing

360 Degree Feedback has become a highly popular form of evaluation in many organizations. It is based on the assumption that
the individuals should be evaluated not simply by their

supervisor, but by everyone who is familiar with or dependent on their work. This may include colleagues, those whom they supervise, customers, outside vendors, and others. The feedback is usually anonymous, as it is assumed that people are more objective under these conditions. Typically, the supervisor of the individual surveys the entire array of evaluations. From an appreciative standpoint, this practice is to be credited for broadening participation in the process. Inclusion is a valuable goal. However, the process can also create a substantial sense of isolation and mistrust; now one must worry not simply about the boss's opinion, but about everyone with whom he or she is in contact. What can be expected from colleagues with whom one is in competition?

From an appreciative standpoint, there are great gains to be achieved through 360 degree *valuing*. Such gains can be achieved at both the individual and group levels. First, consider the various practices suggested for valuing at the individual level. For example, rather than a supervisor expressing what he or she values in a worker, all those with whom the individual works might be asked for such expressions. Or, have the individual speak to all those with whom he is in close contact about the resources he or she brings to the organization. Similarly, in a 360 degree rotation individuals might speak about what support they receive from others. Ideally, in our view, these practices should be dialogic. With mutual sharing, a powerful potential is unleashed for mutual regard and care.

The 360 valuing process may also center on relationships themselves. Rather than focusing on the attributes of individuals, dialogue can shift to explorations of how relationships function best, what it is that is prized about the relationship, or on visions of an ideal relationship. Such dialogues can be initiated through the full circle of one's close working relationships.

****

Two consultants, working in a private organization, were charged with designing a new process for staff evaluation. Since there was a good deal of rivalry among the group, it seemed likely that coming to some sort of collaborative agreement concerning peer evaluation would be a struggle. The consultants decided, after much deliberation, to initiate an appreciative and collaborative form of evaluation on the administrative team, as a way of recruiting their support for an adapted evaluation procedure for the organization's entire staff. The administrative team agreed to participate in this activity.

Over the course of one week, they were given the task of listing what they each believed were their unique contributions to and strengths within the administrative group. They were also asked to make similar, separate lists for each of their colleagues. These lists were delivered to the consultants who combined the lists for each administrative team member. When the team reconvened with the consultants, the walls of the boardroom were covered with the lists — one for each person. Team members were encouraged to move around the room reading each list. (Of course, each person stopped first at his or her own list.)

The conversation that followed this activity was vitalizing. Team members first commented on how many of their colleagues had listed the very same strengths and contributions that they had identified for themselves. This generated a great sense of accomplishment and pride. Then the conversation shifted to those qualities that colleagues attributed to each other but of which members had no self-awareness. For example, one team member was surprised to see that out of his seven colleagues, six of them identified him as offering creative ideas to the group. This team member had not listed creativity as one of his strengths and so was curious to learn that others saw him this way. He was both informed and gratified by their responses.

Finally, the conversation turned to the items each person had listed for him or herself as a strength but that no one else on the team acknowledged. Here, in the silence of omission, was a "gentle" way of expressing what would have been critique under normal evaluation procedures. Yet, in this context of mutual appreciation, what might have been viewed as a critique generated what is better termed a learning conversation.

****

As we see there are numerous practices that enable an organization to move from an orientation of evaluation to valuation — both of individuals and relationships. The horizons are broad and exciting. The appreciative organization moves away from the punitive, depersonalizing practices of evaluation, to practices of valuing that make it possible for organization members at all levels to feel their work is valued and contributive. Initiating valuing processes may be a struggle in traditional organizations. There is no doubt that valuing practices will require ingenuity and dedication to achieve organizational transformational. Valuing must itself become a collective value.

Focus Box

The use of individual evaluation to improve performance is the norm in most organizations. Yet there are negative outcomes to this practice: evaluation creates apprehension, encourages self-preservation at the cost of organizational welfare, creates distance and suspicion among participants, encourages conformity, and reduces contributions to teams.

The challenge is to replace evaluation with a valuing posture in which the emphasis is on valuing individuals and relationships. The result is greater openness in communication, increased trust, an encouragement of creativity, and more enthusiastic participation in collaborative activities. This transformation also helps organizations to become more flexible, information to flow more freely, and decisions to become more sophisticated.

Valuing can be helpful in guiding employees to correct deficit behaviors as a means of enhancing their relationship in the organization. Failures are accepted as a necessary part of growth and creativity. Various practices are described for increased valuing of persons and relationships. For example, on the individual level, inviting people to share what they do well and enjoy in their work, or creating group discussions related to how members can best support one another in their work, can make valuable contributions to organizational life.

Groups can be valued through similar practices, such as inviting team members to share stories of successful group experiences, celebrating group successes, and sharing visions of how the ideal group might function. A strong case is made for 360 degree valuing dialogues.

Chapter 6

Organization in Context:
From Separation to Synchrony

Traditionally we make a clear distinction between an organization and the external world — between an "inside" and an "outside." "We are Penn State" has been a rallying cry of the university for decades. These words suggest that Penn Staters are drawing a boundary around the university — those who are in, and those who are out. For certain purposes, this is certainly a useful distinction: How shall we sustain our growth? Are we balancing our budget? Is the football team going to win the Rose Bowl? These are primarily insider questions, which can best be answered by considering Penn State a separate and distinct entity.

Yet, drawing this dividing line is not always beneficial. The distinction between "us" and "them" can make for adversarial relations. It sets the organization up as a competitor with others in a zero-sum game. If one wins, the other loses. This arrangement also draws the organization into practices that yield suspicion and defensiveness, which ultimately harm the organization itself. Most importantly, the "Big picture," why the organization even exists, may be lost in this atmosphere of antagonism. For example, the mission of a university is to educate. In order to accomplish this greater mission, it is vital to blur boundary distinctions and recognize the fundamental interdependence of the organization with its surrounds — preparatory schools, publishers, the government, news media, public opinion, and so on. More generally, we move from a position of organizations and independent adversaries to an appreciation of interdependence, when we consider that:

- *Every participant within an organization also participates in other groups.* For example, at universities, faculty members are also members of families, clubs, religious groups, and professional organizations. Alumni are scattered throughout the world, and belong to social circles, organizations, and nations that have only a remote connection to their educational institutions. Many Penn State undergraduates go on to graduate schools at other universities. They take their "blue and white" bumper stickers with them when they go. What appears at first glance to be a simple dividing line — whether you are in or out — is blurred.
- *The success of the organization is vitally dependent on the flow of ideas, resources, and actions outside its walls.* If the "outside" is not absorbed into the lifeblood of the organization, over time it ceases to be viable. Every organization, whether a university, a gas station, an art gallery, or a police station, must be coordinated with the environment of which it is a part. If the police station moves to another locale, for example, the Dunkin' Donuts shop may have fewer customers. Although the walls and gates of a physical plant seem fixed and rigid, the life of the organization can only thrive if the actions of those inside the walls are synchronized with all that is exterior to it.

In effect, the organization and environment are profoundly intertwined, and it is essential to nurture relationships in this extended field. For example, developing relationships with people from outside the "old boy" or "old girl" network as consultants, advisors, or as new employees is very significant for an organization, in that these provide a conduit to new ideas, skills, and preferences. These "outsiders" carry the "secrets" of communities developing outside the organization. Without inclusiveness, the fashion world and the entertainment industry, as examples, would be bereft of inspiration and would soon die. When relationships across diverse groups are valued, the potentials for coordination — both within the organization's walls and without are greatly enhanced.

****

Anne Mulcahy, the CEO of Xerox, echoed this view in a recent newspaper interview: "I was lucky to inherit a company in which 'enlightened leaders' long ago had built an infrastructure of recruiting and ... development that has created a diverse team of leaders at the top. I feel fortunate because this is a company that understood the value of inclusiveness before it was in vogue because it believed it was the best way to keep talent."

****

Appreciating the Surrounds: A Case Study

As we are emphasizing, the appreciative organization does not move *against* a resistant world, but *with* it in a way that all may benefit. The following story illuminates the potentials:

****

Sixty years ago the military services had acquired a great deal of land on which to train its troops and test its equipment. Often this land was in sparsely populated parts of the US and its territories. In Puerto Rican waters, for example, the US Navy had possession of 70% of a tropical island, called Vieques, since 1941. On this island, they held target practice with live ammunition, practiced "war games," and tested radioactive depleted uranium shells. Eventually Puerto Rican activists and sympathetic mainlanders raised such a clamor that the Navy had to take notice. However, the reaction of the Navy was one of distain, arrogance, and insistence upon its right to continue to carry out its mission. Media interests exploited this David and Goliath story to the hilt, and eventually in May 2003, the Navy was forced to vacate the island, which today has become a new honeymoon destination.

The Department of Defense has now adopted a new and more appreciative orientation. Top policy makers are seeking ways to facilitate collaborative interchanges between local communities and their own need to train soldiers and test equipment. In one successful effort, funds from a base were donated to the Nature Conservancy so that woodlands and wetlands nearby could be purchased and maintained. This provided a buffer between the base and the community, a win-win situation for all — including nature.

****

Steps toward Coordination in Context

What steps can be taken to help an organization become more resilient, flexible, and responsive to its environment? We suggest the following means for enhancing coordination:

Multiple Channels of Communication

As a first step toward coordination, it is important to open as many channels of communication as possible. In this way, the organization begins to appreciate the sea of meanings in which it resides. How is the organization being constructed by those who are in a position to evaluate it and contribute to its welfare? It is especially critical that the voices that are antagonistic or competitive are included, along with the group's supporters. It is helpful to hear those who are served by the organization, as well as those who service and supply its needs. Communications from the business community, civic organizations, lobbyists, public opinion polls, media resources, governmental policy makers, and international sources more generally are relevant.

Appreciative Listening

While opening diverse channels of communication is an important beginning, a special habit of appreciative listening must be developed. In listening appreciatively, we strive to understand why it is important for people to express themselves as they do. What is at stake for them? What values and traditions are being represented? Where does the future lie for this constituency? Through this form of listening, we gain a sense of the legitimacy of what is being said from the point of view of the speakers. The result is the kind of respect and knowledge out of which coordination can emerge (see also Chapter 2).

It should also be noted that silence is itself a form of speech. If one can develop the skill of noticing the spaces when no affirmations are given or personal preferences expressed, then one might suspect that alternative constructions are being entertained, but not brought into the conversation. Listening appreciatively should allow the unspoken voices, those who are reluctant to join the conversation, to be heard.

Framing Fruitful Questions

Another important step in generating a collaborative flow of communication is to consider how questions are framed. In *Change Your Questions, Change Your Life*, Marilee Adams argues that success in organization and family life can be strongly influenced by the type of questions that people pose to one another. A question, such as "Who is responsible for this mess?" will lead most listeners to duck and run, if possible, or engage in a "cover up" story. Rather, a question that is framed out of curiosity in the same situation, such as "How do you think we created this situation?" could reduce defensiveness, reduce the tendency to blame anyone, and lead to a fruitful discussion. Two other questions could bear different fruit: "How can we turn this situation into a win-win?" and "What can we learn from what happened?" This last question points up an important issue. Clearly one's acceptance that mistakes happen, that some mistakes aren't mistakes at all, and that everything can have a value of some sort are helpful steps in the direction of appreciative organizing.

Creating Open Communication

In a thriving organization, open communication should be pursued despite differences and difficulties. The classic case of frankness and corporate transparency occurred in the 1980s when Johnson & Johnson recalled all packages of Tylenol after tampering was discovered in a few bottles. While it was a financial setback at the time, the gain in public trust and confidence in the company continued long after the incident left the front pages.

Many companies have followed their lead, ultimately benefiting from the forthright handling of the situation. Another interesting case at the moment involves the cigarette company, Philip Morris, which is attempting to create positive connections with diverse constituents, including those who are strong critics of smoking and cigarette manufacturers. The goal of the company is to shed its image as the devil in a cellophane package, and to find some credibility and accommodation among those external to the company. Through open communications, the organization hopes that diverse views can be explored, their significance revealed, and new ground broken toward a more positive relationship. Importantly, opinions and ideas are understood in context; they are attached to full human beings.

Turning Conflict to Cooperation

Most organizations will find outsiders who are antagonistic to its efforts. Such expressions should not be devalued. These messages are particularly useful in alerting an organization to points of vulnerability. However, rather than simply acknowledging antagonism and understanding why it exists, efforts to move toward more viable forms of relationship are essential to the appreciative organization. To do so is to invite participation in productive conversation and inclusion instead of unproductive antagonism. At times, such a movement can be invited through the kind of productive dialogue just described. Appreciative Inquiry can be an especially effective means of transforming antagonism to cooperation. However, there is no limit to creative alternatives.

****

In one impressive case, an organization was being picketed by an anti-vivisectionist group that decried their research practices. There was no means of reaching accord on the basic issues at stake. However, rather than stimulating greater antagonism, the organization invited the demonstrating group to join them in mounting a public exhibit in which both sides of the issue would be represented. Antagonism was replaced by mutual exploration. Members of the two groups also worked together effectively and appreciatively. Importantly, the organization later developed an internal group to represent the demonstrators' views in their meetings.

****

Enhancing Global Relations through Technology

The explosion in electronic communication — email, cell phones, tele-conferencing, websites, and the like — generate major new challenges for the organization. In particular, there is a strong tendency for organizations to spread globally. At Citibank, for example, an American network engineer may need to simultaneously coordinate activities with colleagues in Hungary, Columbia, and the Philippines, despite differences of time and cultural expectations. The lack of face-to-face relations in these contexts poses a special challenge. Nonverbal signals, which carry with them important signs of affect, are missing, and therefore, expressions of value and affirmation may be lacking. Also at issue are matters of trust and competency, which may be evaluated differently in various cultures. All too often, when people work together at a distance, organizational members begin to see each other as "outsiders." They trust and understand locally, yet the voice on the other end of Skype seems alien.

****

Research conducted at the University of Michigan School of Business found that when organizational members met with each other before working as a team at a distance, they were much more productive than such teams composed of members who had never met. Through talking about everyday matters, sharing meals, engaging in leisure activities, and just hanging out, people seem to develop a sense of trust, common purpose, and identification with one another. These sentiments grease the wheels of future relations. The person who shared your taste in fine art or ball games, who helped you out in a puzzling situation, or loaned you her cell phone can be assumed to be a worthy teammate, even if your views on a particular topic diverge. Doubt gives way to the benefit of the doubt. Productive dialogue begins here.

****

In his volume, *Appreciative Sharing of Knowledge*, Tojo Thatchenkery outlines a practice of particular relevance to these conditions. He arranges for pairs of participants to share stories of successful relating. They might tell stories of successful knowledge sharing, a close friendship with someone they have never met, or a time when they went the extra mile to bring about successful coordination. Such stories not only create a context for developing mutual trust but, generate optimism regarding the future. As well, they demonstrate specific practices that can contribute to effective coordination. As the research suggests, it would be optimal if these exchanges were conducted in a face-to-face setting. However, through technology it is also possible that wider sharing among groups could take place and resourceful archives established.

In terms of the global context, especially via the internet, we find it useful to think of *knowledge webs*, that is, broadly arrayed conversations that continuously yield new knowledge and insight through conversations being carried on by participants from many locales. If creativity results from the novel combination of two or more elements, then the knowledge web is an enormous font of creative potential. The vitality and coordinating capabilities of the global organization may well depend on participation in extended webs of knowledge. While there are many complexities in coordinating across continents, the power that comes when the resources of this vast network are linked in a coordinated manner, serves to enhance the productivity of multi-national enterprises. In an appreciative organization, open dialogue across organizational boundaries is a key to relational growth and organizational health.

Focus Box

The focus of this chapter is on the insider/outsider distinction, which often defines an organization. There are limits to maintaining strong boundaries because:

1. Every participant within an organization also belongs to others,
2. Organizations require the flow of resources across its boundaries to be sustained, and
3. The organization and the environment are interdependently created.

Organizations can increase cross-boundary coordination by opening multiple channels of communication, nurturing sensitive dialogue, framing fruitful questions; and creating open communication.

Potential antagonisms with outside groups may be defused through joining in collaborative efforts. Here there is a merging of inside/outside. In the global organization, dispersed wings can become outsiders to each other. Here it is useful to supplement the distance communication process with early face-to-face contact. Sharing stories of success can be effective in building trust and optimism. Internet communications are also vital in building knowledge webs that span space and time limitations. Coordinated effectively they add power to the potentials of international organizations.

In Conclusion — An Offering

As the twenty-first century unfolds, the call for appreciative organizing is gaining strength. A greater openness to new ways of working together is developing. Traditional forms of organizing no longer function in optimal ways. Top-down authority structures that have historically dominated public life are inadequate to meet the challenges of rapidly accumulating information, workplace diversity, rapid shifts in public opinion, and shifting tensions in the geo-political context. Change must come. As authors, we offer the resources in this book in hopes that creative and beneficial outcomes may emerge in diverse organizational settings. Our experience gives us optimism regarding the potentials of an appreciative orientation. However, we do not consider these views as a fixed and final pronouncement on organizing. Rather we envision this volume as an opening to new conversations, new insights, and innovative practices. Every organization is unique and the conditions of organizational life are continuously in motion. It is our hope, however, that this book can open new possibilities for all.

Glossary

Chapter 1: Toward Appreciative Organizing

Appreciative Inquiry (AI): A form of inquiry that seeks the "positive core" in an organization, relationship, or person. It serves as the basis of many interventions by consultants in organizations, and is frequently done as a whole system collaborative activity. The roots of AI are found in social constructionism.

Appreciative Organization: An organization that depends upon an Appreciative Inquiry approach for its sustenance and growth. The organization is viewed as a repository of life-giving relationships. Leaders encourage webs of relatedness, dialogue, multiple realities, openness, imaginary, as well as collaborative action.

Command and Control Organization: A hierarchically arranged organization that is structured along military lines, in which orders pass from top to bottom. Also see "traditional" organization.

CEO: Chief Executive Officer, regarded as the head of a traditional organization, who provides the vision and goals, authorizes decisions, and leads the organization in its endeavors. Often regarded as a heroic figure.

Social Constructionism: A theoretical framework that stresses the importance of communities of people engaging in interaction to provide meaning, value and a sense of reality to ongoing activities and events.

Traditional Organizations: Organizations established as solid hierarchical structures, pyramidal in form. Orders move from top to bottom, information is passed in the opposite direction. Participants function as individuals in competition for upward movement. Firm boundaries separate the organization from the world outside.

Chapter 2: Appreciation in the Meaning-Making Process

Conversational Partnerships: Forms of conversational relationships in which an appreciative process brings forth trust, openness, and understanding. Positive listening invites the other into a conversational partnership.

Co-Construction of Meaning: Meaning is created through the joint actions of people engaged with one another, not as a private, personal event.

The Posture of "Not-knowing": In conversation, being provisional about one's own views, offering responses in a tentative manner. Giving others time and space for expression.

Monologic Conversation: A conversation in which individuals do not listen to one another. Speakers tend to defend and sharpen their own positions against others.

Multiple Selves: Because we participate in an unprecedented array of relationships, real or mediated, we carry with us multiple and conflicting ideas, insights, and rationalities. These various viewpoints can be described metaphorically as multiple selves.

Narratives: Stories that construct the past in ways that present more possibility for newness in the task at hand and in the organization. Stories fortify ongoing relationships, lending them value or importance. Stories track the history of an organization and help to create its identity.

Positive Listening: Listening that allows the others in conversation to fully express their views without interruption, offering responses non-judgmentally, and using paraphrases to avoid misunderstandings.

Relational Equality: When all people in the conversation have an equal right to contribute to the conversation with equal respect.

Transformative Dialogue: An interactive conversational process in which the combination of meanings are created by the participants creating a new outcome — one that none could have predicted at the start of the conversation.

Valuing the Other: Honoring the willingness of another to enter into conversation.

Chapter 3: Leadership as Collaborative Participation

Collaborative Participation: Specific practices of seeking (co-creation?) that make it possible to discover differences, highlighting unique strengths and abilities, and bringing out the best of people in relation to each other.

"Great Man" Theory of Leadership: Leaders are assumed to possess special capacities and skills that set them apart from ordinary people and make them highly qualified to direct the activities of others. Usually assumed to be a heroic man, e.g. Abraham Lincoln.

Leaders: Those who are willing to serve as the relational conduit for inquiry and action; and who effectively invite others into relationships that organize energy, effort, and action toward mutually determined ends.

Leadership: In the appreciative organization leadership depends upon collaborative participation. Leadership emerges from patterns of relationship. Appreciative leadership can be exercised at every level of an organization.

Relational Resonance: Being attuned to the "vibes" coalescing and dissolving around one.

Chapter 4: Appreciative Organizing in Action: Small Groups and the "AI" Summit

Anticipatory Principle: Decisions and actions are based not only on past experiences but also on what we anticipate in the future.

Appreciative Inquiry Summit: Large group planning method often accomplished with the total membership of the organization in which face-to-face sessions are facilitated over three to four days. Meetings result in more dialogues and creative visioning, as well as better internal logic and higher energy release.

Constructionist Principle: The acceptance of the social constructionist stance toward reality and social knowledge.

Poetic Principle: The valuing of story telling as a sensitive way of gathering holistic information about the organization, including the affective component of the experience.

Positive Principle: A belief that a positive approach to any issue is a valid and fruitful basis for action more so than a negative approach. When we focus on the positive, the positive then strengthens as a system or situation grows.

Principle of Simultaneity: A realization that **inquiry is change**; the questions we ask are fateful in that an organization will turn its energy in the direction of a question, whether positive or negative; as a result, the seeds of change are embedded in the formulation of a question.

Self-Organization: Non-directive activity in which group members create their own internal organization, which is separated from the major organization to which they belong, where they use their own resources and implement their own decisions, based on their own images of the future.

Chapter 5: Evaluation to Valuation

Evaluation: An assessment to determine or fix the significance, worth, or condition of something, often in comparison to a fixed standard or to other people. Current processes of evaluation of people and performance are often viewed as stressful events.

Generativity: Forms of relational engagement that enable, facilitate, and promote ways of "going on together." The ability or power to create or produce something that activates more creation of possibilities — again and again.

Valuing: A contrast to Evaluation, in that it is a focus on that which the employee, group, or organization does that is esteemed or desired by the organization.

360 Degree Valuation: A form of dialogic practice in which conversations are developed on the valuing of relationships surrounding each person in an organization (hence the circular notion of 360 degrees). For example, the mail clerk might have dialogues with the manager, those who receive the mail, and the postal worker who delivers the mail to the organization.

Chapter 6: Organization in Context:
From Separation to Synchrony

Appreciative Listening: Looking for, hearing, and acknowledging the more positive possibilities in the speeches and dialogues that are offered.

Knowledge Webs: Broadly arrayed conversations carried out by participants from many locales. Through these interconnections, new forms of knowledge become possible.

Multiple Channels of Communication: A variety of forms of media that carry similar messages through different channels, e.g. website and email messages on the same topic.

Positive Linguistic Framings: Putting the best possible verbal "face" on some event, policy, tactic, and so on.

Suggested Readings and Resources

The authors have compiled this list of suggested readings to further the exploration and learning about the appreciative organization and appreciative organizing.

Chapter 1

Barrett, F. & Fry, R. (2005). *Appreciative Inquiry: A Positive Approach to Building Cooperative Capacity*. Chagrin Falls, Ohio: Taos Institute Publications.

Gergen, K.J. & Gergen, M. (2004). *Social Construction, Entering the Dialogue*. Chagrin Falls, Ohio: Taos Institute Publications.

Gergen, K. J. (2001). *An Invitation to Social Constructionism*. London, Thousand Oaks, California: Sage.

Morgan, G. (2006). *Images of Organization*. London, Thousand Oaks, California: Sage. (updated edition). (Originally published in 1998.)

Sawyer, R.K. (2003). *Group Creativity, Music, Theater, Collaboration*. Mahwah, New Jersey: Erlbaum.

Seiling, J. (2005). *Moving from Individual to Constructive Accountability*. Unpublished Doctoral Dissertation, *Tilburg University*, available at: www.TaosInstitute.net.

Stavros, J. & Torres, C. (2005). *Dynamic Relationships: Unleashing the Power of Apprecitive Inquiry in Daily Living.* Chagrin Falls, Ohio: Taos Institute Publications.

Straus, D. (2002). *How to Make Collaboration Work.* San Francisco: Berrett-Koehler.

Weick, K. (1995). *Sensemaking in Organizations.* Thousand Oaks, California: Sage.

Chapter 2

Ackoff, R. L. (1999). *Ackoff's Best: His Classic Writings on Management.* New York: John Wiley.

Anderson, H. (1997). *Conversation, Language and Possibilities: A Postmodern Approach to Psychotherapy.* New York: Basic Books.

Anderson, H. (2005). The myth of not-knowing. *Family Process*, *44*, 497-504.

Anderson, H. & D. Gehart (Eds.) (2006). *Collaborative Therapy: Relationships and Conversations that Make a Difference.* New York: Routledge.

De Bono, E. (1999). *Six Thinking Hats.* Boston: Back Bay. (Originally published in 1985.)

McNamee, S. & Gergen, K. J. & others (1998). *Relational Responsibility: A Transformative Dialogue.* Thousand Oaks, California: Sage.

Phillips, N., & Hardy, C. (2002). *Discourse Analysis: Investigating Processes of Social Construction.* Thousand Oaks, California: Sage.

Chapter 3

Boyatzis, R. & McKee, A. (2005). *Resonant Leadership: Renewing Yourself and Connecting with Others through Mindfulness, Hope, and Compassion.* Cambridge, Massachusetts: Harvard Business School Publishing.

Chrislip, D. and Larson, C. (1994). *Collaborative Leadership: How Citizens and Civic Leaders Can Make a Difference.* San Francisco: Jossey-Bass.

Depree, M. (1992). *Leadership Jazz*. New York: Dell Publishing.

Drath, W. (2001). *Deep Blue Sea: Rethinking the Source of Leadership*. San Francisco: Jossey-Bass.

Hackman, R. (2002). *Leading Teams: Setting the Stage for Great Performances*. Boston: Harvard Business School Press.

Pearce, C. L., & Conger, J. A. (2003). *Shared Leadership*. Thousand Oaks, California: Sage.

Raelin, J. (2003). *Creating Leaderful Organizations: How to Bring Out Leadership in Everyone*. San Francisco: Berrett-Kohler.

Schiller, M., Holland, B-M, & Riley, D. (Eds.) (2001). *Appreciative Leaders: In the Eye of the Beholder*. Chagrin Falls, Ohio: Taos Institute Publications.

Spillane, J. P. (2006). *Distributed Leadership*. San Francisco: John Wiley.

Srivastva, S., Cooperrider, D. L., and Associates (1990) *Appreciative Management and Leadership: The Power of Positive Thought and Action in Organizations*. San Francisco, California: Jossey-Bass.

Wheatley, M. (1992). *Leadership and the New Science*. San Francisco: Berrett-Koehler.

Whitney, D., & Ludema, J. (2007). *Appreciative Leadership Development Program*. Corporation for Positive Change.

www.aipractitioner.com (newsletter with several issues related to leadership)

Chapter 4

Barrett, F. J., & Fry, R. E. (2005). *Appreciative Inquiry: A Positive Approach to Building Cooperative Capacity*. Chagrin Falls, Ohio: Taos Institute Publishing.

Cooperrider, D. & Avital, M. (Eds.) (2004). *Advances in AI: Constructive Discourse and Human Organization*. New York: Elsevier.

Ludema, J. D., Whitney, D. , Mohr, B., Griffin T. J. (2003). *The Appreciative Inquiry Summit: A Practitioner's Guide for Leading Large-Group Change*. San Francisco: Berrett-Koehler.

Watkins, J., & Mohr, B. (2001). *Appreciative Inquiry: Change at the Speed of Imagination*. San Francisco: Jossey Bass Pfeiffer.

Whitney, D., & Trosten-Bloom, A. (2003). *The Power of Appreciative Inquiry: A Practical Guide to Positive Change*. San Francisco: Berrett-Koehler.

AI Commons website devoted to the fullest sharing of AI resources, tools, case studies and more: http://appreciativeinquiry.case.edu/.

Chapter 5

Bambino, D. (2002). Critical Friends, *Educational Leadership*. March, pp. 25-27.

Dunne, F., Nave, B., Lewis, A. (December, 2000). Critical Friends Groups: Teachers Helping Teachers to Improve Student Learning. *Phi Delta Kappa Center for Evaluation, Development, and Research Bulletin*, No. 28.

McNamee, S. (2006). *Appreciative Evaluation in an Educational Context: Inviting Conversations of Assessment and Development*. In D.M. Hosking and S. McNamee (Eds.), *The Social Construction of Organization* (pp. 211-224), Malmo, Sweden: Liber and Copenhagen Business School Press.

Pearce, C. L. & Confer, J. A. (Eds.). (2003). *Shared Leadership: Reframing the Hows and Whys of Leadership*. London, Thousand Oaks, California: Sage.

Preskill, H. and Tzavaras Catsambas, T. (2006). *Reframing Evaluation through Appreciative Inquiry*. London: Sage Publications.

Whitney, D. and Trosten-Bloom (2002). *Positive Change at Work*. Cleveland, Ohio: Lakeshore Communications.

AI Practitioner: February 2005 Issue: Applying AI to Evaluation Practice, see: www.aipractitioner.com.

Chapter 6

Adams, M. (2004). *Change Your Questions, Change Your Life. 7 Powerful Tools for Life and Work*. San Francisco, California: Berrett-Koehler.

Ghemawat, P. (2007). *Redefining Global Strategy: Crossing Borders in a World Where Differences still Matter*. Boston: Harvard Business School Press.

Holman, P. & Devane, T. (Eds.) (1999). *The Change Handbook: Group Methods for Shaping the Future*. San Francisco: Berrett-Koehler Publishers.

Isaacs, W. (1999). *Dialogue and the Art of Thinking Together*. New York: Doubleday, A Currency Book.

Lord, J., with P. McAllister, (2007). *What Kind of World Do You Want? Here's How We Can Get It*. Private Publication, reviewed at www.whatkindofworld.com.

Rosenberg, Marshall (2005). *Speak Peace in a World of Conflict: What You Say Next Will Change Your World*. Encinitas, California: Puddle Jumper Press.

Senge, P. (1990). *The Fifth Discipline: The Art and Practice of the Learning Organization*. New York: Currency Doubleday.

Vogt, E. E., Brown, J., & Isaacs, D. (2003). *The Art of Powerful Questions: Catalyzing Insight, Innovation, and Action*. Waltham, Massachusetts: Pegasus Communications, Inc. www.pegasuscom.com.

Visit *Imagine Chicago* to learn more about community development and collaboration: www.imaginechicago.org.